# Historical Maps of Ireland

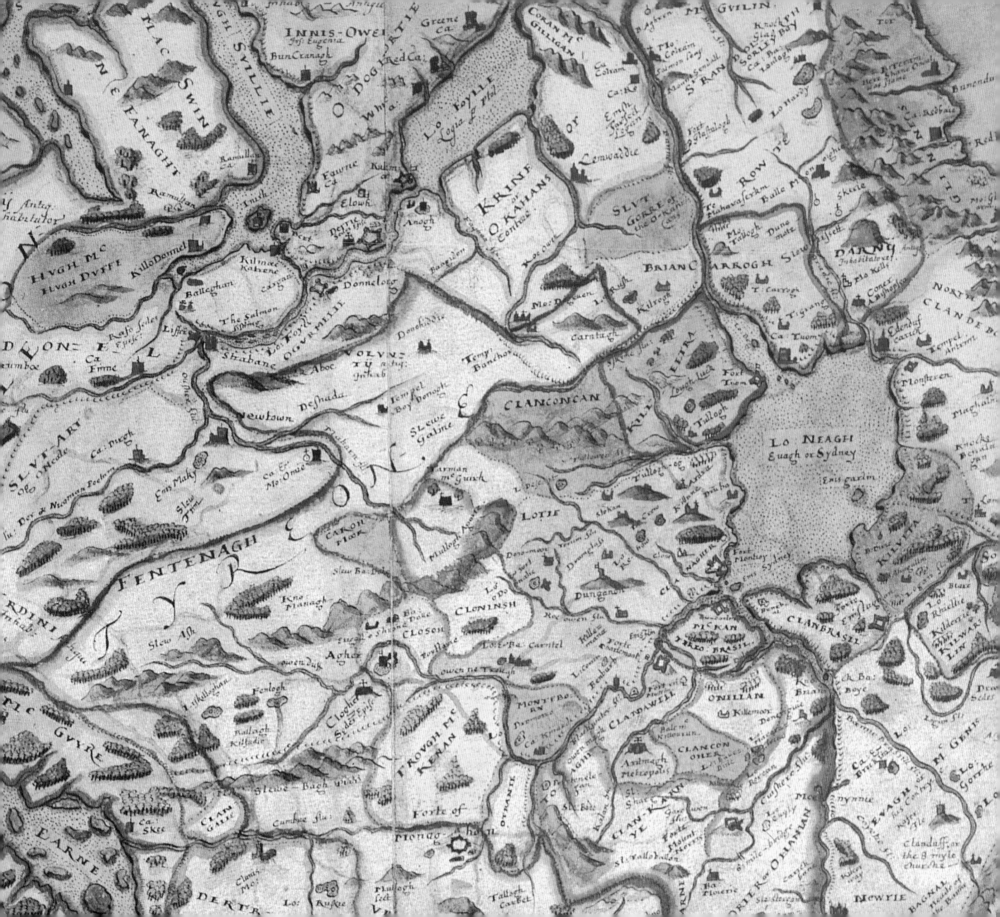

# Historical Maps of Ireland

Michael Swift

CHARTWELL
BOOKS, INC.

## Acknowledgments

The Public Records Office was the source of all the maps used in this book.

Crown Copyright material in the Public Record Office is reproduced by permission of the Controller of Her Majesty's Stationery Office.

Images are reproduced by courtesy of the Public Record Office.

This edition published in 1999 by
CHARTWELL BOOKS, INC.
A division of BOOK SALES, INC
114 Northfield Avenue,
Edison, New Jersey 08837

Produced by
PRC Publishing Ltd,
Kiln House, 210 New Kings Road, London SW6 4NZ

© 1999 PRC Publishing Ltd.

ISBN 0 78581 109 5

Printed and bound in China

# contents

**Introduction**    **6**

Celtic Ireland . . . . . . . . . . . . . 6
Arrival of the Normans . . . . . . . . . 7
The 16th Century . . . . . . . . . . . . 9
Ireland Under the Stuarts . . . . . . . 11
Years Leading to the Act of Union . . 12
Period of the Union . . . . . . . . . . 13
Easter Rising and its Aftermath . . . . 15
Civil War . . . . . . . . . . . . . . . 16
Republic after the Civil War . . . . . 17
Northern Ireland after Partition . . . 18

**The Cartography**

Reasons for Cartography . . . . . . . . 19
Development of Cartography . . . . . 19
About the Maps . . . . . . . . . . . . 20
Place Names . . . . . . . . . . . . . . 20
Measurements . . . . . . . . . . . . . 21

**The Maps**

Ireland c.1558 . . . . . . . . . . . . . 22
Bantry Bay c1558 . . . . . . . . . . . 22
Ireland 1567 . . . . . . . . . . . . . . 22
Belfast Lough 1569 . . . . . . . . . . 24
County Down c.1570 . . . . . . . . . 24
Newry c.1570 . . . . . . . . . . . . . 26
Newry c.1570 . . . . . . . . . . . . . 26
Newry c.1570 . . . . . . . . . . . . . 26
Corkbeg Fort c.1571 . . . . . . . . . . 27
Munster c.1572 . . . . . . . . . . . . 29
Castlemaine 1572 . . . . . . . . . . . 29
Wicklow 1579 . . . . . . . . . . . . . 30
Munster c.1580 . . . . . . . . . . . . 30
Ulster c.1580 . . . . . . . . . . . . . 30
Ireland c.1580 . . . . . . . . . . . . . 33
County Down c.1580 . . . . . . . . . 33
Antrim c.1580 . . . . . . . . . . . . . 34

Portrush c.1580 . . . . . . . . . . . . 34
Idrone c.1580 . . . . . . . . . . . . . 35
Smerwick Harbor 1580 . . . . . . . . 36
Roscommon 1581 . . . . . . . . . . . 36
County Mayo 1585 . . . . . . . . . . 36
Cork and Kerry 1587 . . . . . . . . . 37
Limerick 1587 . . . . . . . . . . . . . 39
Limerick 1587 . . . . . . . . . . . . . 39
Mayo 1587 . . . . . . . . . . . . . . . 41
Tralee 1587 . . . . . . . . . . . . . . 41
Blackwater Fort 1587 . . . . . . . . . 42
Sligo 1589 . . . . . . . . . . . . . . . 42
Monaghan 1590 . . . . . . . . . . . . 45
Cavan 1591 . . . . . . . . . . . . . . . 45
Monaghan 1591 . . . . . . . . . . . . 47
Enniskillen 1594 . . . . . . . . . . . . 47
Banagher c.1600 . . . . . . . . . . . . 48
Carrickfergus c.1600 . . . . . . . . . . 48
Ulster 1602-3 . . . . . . . . . . . . . 48
Ulster 1602-3 . . . . . . . . . . . . . 51
Ulster 1602-3 . . . . . . . . . . . . . 51
Clanawley c.1609 . . . . . . . . . . . 53
Clankee c.1609 . . . . . . . . . . . . 53
Clankelly c.1609 . . . . . . . . . . . . 54
Dungannon c.1609 . . . . . . . . . . 57
Knockninny c.1609 . . . . . . . . . . 58
Knockninny c.1609 . . . . . . . . . . 58
Loughtee c.1609 . . . . . . . . . . . . 61
Omagh c.1609 . . . . . . . . . . . . . 61
Oneilland c.1609 . . . . . . . . . . . 62
Strabane 1609 . . . . . . . . . . . . . 62
Tullyhaw c.1609 . . . . . . . . . . . . 62
Ireland c.1610 . . . . . . . . . . . . . 65
Augher c.1610 . . . . . . . . . . . . . 66
Charlemont c.1610 . . . . . . . . . . 66
Mulline c.1610 . . . . . . . . . . . . . 66
Monaghan/Enislaghan c.1610 . . . . 67
Kinsale 1637 . . . . . . . . . . . . . . 68

Boyne 1690 . . . . . . . . . . . . . . . 69
Kinsale 1691 . . . . . . . . . . . . . . 70
Dublin 1722 . . . . . . . . . . . . . . 70
Lower Iveagh 1725 . . . . . . . . . . 72
Ireland c.1759 . . . . . . . . . . . . . 72
Lismore 1760 . . . . . . . . . . . . . 75
Cork c.1770 . . . . . . . . . . . . . . 75
Kinsale c.1770 . . . . . . . . . . . . . 76
Cork 1781 . . . . . . . . . . . . . . . 76
Dublin c.1790 . . . . . . . . . . . . . 79
Ireland 1793 . . . . . . . . . . . . . . 80
Londonderry 1799 . . . . . . . . . . 81
Cork 1800/1802 . . . . . . . . . . . . 83
Dublin c.1800 . . . . . . . . . . . . . 83
Dublin 1801 . . . . . . . . . . . . . . 84
Cork 1803 . . . . . . . . . . . . . . . 84
Dublin 1803 . . . . . . . . . . . . . . 86
Dublin 1803 . . . . . . . . . . . . . . 86
Dublin 1803 . . . . . . . . . . . . . . 87
Enniskillen District 1803 . . . . . . . 88
Ireland 1803 . . . . . . . . . . . . . . 89
Limerick 1803 . . . . . . . . . . . . . 91
Lough Swilly 1803 . . . . . . . . . . . 91
New Ross 1803 . . . . . . . . . . . . 93
Spike Island 1803 . . . . . . . . . . . 93
Ireland 1804 . . . . . . . . . . . . . . 94
Cork 1809 . . . . . . . . . . . . . . . 96
Ballincollig 1810 . . . . . . . . . . . 96
Banagher 1810 . . . . . . . . . . . . . 99
Hollymount 1810 . . . . . . . . . . . 99
Howth 1810 . . . . . . . . . . . . . . 100
Meelick 1810 . . . . . . . . . . . . . . 101
Shannonbridge 1810 . . . . . . . . . 103
Ballincollig 1811 . . . . . . . . . . . 103
Carrickfergus 1811 . . . . . . . . . . 104
Charlemont 1811 . . . . . . . . . . . 105
Cork 1812 . . . . . . . . . . . . . . . 106
Dublin 1814/15 . . . . . . . . . . . . 107

Charlemont 1815 . . . . . . . . . . . 108
Kinsale 1815 . . . . . . . . . . . . . . 108
Dunleary 1820 . . . . . . . . . . . . . 111
Baltimore 1821 . . . . . . . . . . . . 111
Carlingford Lough 1821 . . . . . . . 113
Newton Hamilton 1821 . . . . . . . 113
Sligo 1821 . . . . . . . . . . . . . . . 115
Carrickfergus 1822 . . . . . . . . . . 115
Clonoe 1822 . . . . . . . . . . . . . . 116
Culmore 1825 . . . . . . . . . . . . . 117
Waterford 1825 . . . . . . . . . . . . 118
Templemore 1826/31 . . . . . . . . . 120
Charlemont District 1827 . . . . . . 120
Londonderry 1827 . . . . . . . . . . 122
Dublin District 1828 . . . . . . . . . 122
Carlingford Lough 1831 . . . . . . . 125
Dublin 1831 . . . . . . . . . . . . . . 125
Dunmore East 1832 . . . . . . . . . . 127
Southwest Ireland 1837 . . . . . . . 128
Dublin 1837 . . . . . . . . . . . . . . 131
Dublin 1837 . . . . . . . . . . . . . . 131
Ballinrobe 1838 . . . . . . . . . . . . 133
Lower Malone 1840 . . . . . . . . . . 133
Dublin 1843-44 . . . . . . . . . . . . 135
Belfast 1846 . . . . . . . . . . . . . . 135
Ireland c.1846 . . . . . . . . . . . . . 137
Newry, Warren Point & Rostrevor
    Railway, 1846 . . . . . . . . . . . 138
Belfast 1847 . . . . . . . . . . . . . . 138
Portrush c.1859 . . . . . . . . . . . . 141
Ireland c.1865 . . . . . . . . . . . . . 143

**index of maps**    **144**

# *INTRODUCTION*

INTRODUCT

Ireland, or Eire in the Irish language, is affectionately referred to as the Emerald Isle. It is the second largest of the group of islands known collectively as the British Isles. The island has an area of 32,600 square miles of which 27,100 now form the Republic of Ireland and 5,500 the Province of Northern Ireland. The island possesses a coastline of almost 2,000 miles. The relative populations are 3.5 million and 1.6 million respectively.

Although the first evidence of settlement occurs some 7,000 years ago, when the first settlers migrated westwards from Scotland and settled initially in the region known in the future as Antrim, it was some 4,500 years later — when the Celtic tribes first started to arrive — that true Irish history started.

It is not the place of this book to examine in depth the causes and consequences of the often tempestuous relationship between the various races of the British Isles. Suffice it to note that it is impossible to discuss the various maps illustrated in this book without reference to the tensions that have existed — and indeed continue to exist — among the different traditions within Ireland.

The history of the island of Ireland is not a happy one. Famine, population loss, civil war, murder, colonization, and terrorism all feature. But, as the island approaches the new Millennium, there are now greater causes for optimism — both among the five million people of the island and also among the many millions world-wide who can claim an Irish ancestry. Many of the troubles are now behind it. The Republic of Ireland is now the fastest growing economy within the European Union; for the first time in the island's history there are now more arrivals than departures among the population. In Northern Ireland, the peace process seems to be bringing progress, however slowly and tenuously, and an increasing recognition that there is space within the country for a recognition of the separate traditions of Unionism and Nationalism.

## *Celtic Ireland*

The date of the actual Celtic arrival in Ireland is uncertain, but it probably occurred in the second half of the last Millennium BC. There were existing populations in Ireland — Neolithic and Bronze Age — and it is clear that these earlier civilizations had an impact upon the newcomers. The Irish language, for example, owes much to the existing population as do many of the traditional legends. As elsewhere, when there was a migration of people, the original population found itself subsumed into the ranks of the newcomers.

The arrival of the Celts was but part of a massive population shift that occurred throughout Europe at this time. One factor behind this was the growth of the Roman Empire; although Rome conquered England, Wales and southern Scotland, the north of Scotland and Ireland remained unconquered. The Romans, however, were not unaware of the presence of Ireland — or Hibernia — as it was known to them and there is considerable evidence of trading between Roman Britain and Celtic Ireland.

As Roman influence in Britain — as elsewhere — gradually declined under the threat from the so-called "barbarian" tribes in the 4th century AD, so the Irish (and the Picts from Scotland) commenced raids into Britain. A major foray in AD376 was a precursor to the final demise of Roman Britain in the early 5th century AD. Following on from these raids, the Irish started to colonize much of western Britain; there were particularly important Irish settlements established in South Wales, Devon and Cornwall. Further north, in the future Scotland, the Irish created the Kingdom of Dal Riata; in the 9th century AD this kingdom defeated the Picts, thereby creating the Kingdom of Scotland.

One consequence of the close relations with Roman Britain was the arrival of Christianity. The first missionaries arrived in Ireland in the late 4th century AD — probably from Gaul (France) — and the first verifiable date in the Christian conversion of Ireland comes in AD431 when Palladius, a cleric from Auxerre, was sent as a bishop. The most famous of these early missionaries, and later the patron saint of Ireland, was St Patrick. In the mid-5th century AD, Patrick was captured in England as a 16-year-old by pagans and taken to Ireland for a life of slavery. Eventually he escaped and was later to return to Ireland as a missionary. At this time Irish Christianity was heavily influenced by Britain, particularly in

the creation of monasteries and in the lack of a centralized ecclesiastical structure. A further consequence of the arrival of Christianity was improved learning and new laws. Armagh became the center of Irish Christianity as a result of its close links with St Patrick.

While Ireland retained its Christianity through the Dark Ages, the result of the pagan invasion of Roman Britain — the arrival of the Angles, Saxons and Jutes from northern Europe — was to extinguish Christianity in Britain. It was from Ireland that Christianity was gradually reintroduced to Scotland — through the missionary work of, for example, St Columba based at Iona. England was reconverted by the work of Catholic missionaries from Rome leading to two distinct traditions in the British Isles with, for example, different dates for the celebration of Easter. The Celtic traditions of Christianity, inevitably divorced from the mainstream Catholic church, survived until the Synod of Whitby in AD669 when the Catholic tradition triumphed.

During the period of Celtic dominance, the population of Ireland fluctuated between 0.5 and 1 million; the numbers varying according to disease and famine. The island was not a single entity, but comprised numerous small fiefdoms — some 80 to 100 kingdoms have been identified. But gradually many of these smaller units became dependent upon overlords and some five or six provincial kings came to dominate. There were the inevitable dynastic struggles, although no single overall monarch was to emerge. One of the dominant clans — the Uí Néill dynasty — claimed overlordship (the legendary "Kingship of Tara," which predated the Celtic arrival) but was unable to impose it.

From the end of the 8th century a further military threat to the Celts came with the first appearance of the Viking raiders from Scandinavia. The Vikings burned Rathlin in 795 and three years later destroyed the monastery on St Patrick's Island. In 807 further forays destroyed Inishmurray and Roscam and this set a pattern. In the 830s, the invasions became more intense — in 837, for example, 60 ships were to be found on the River Boyne and another 60 on the Liffey with the Viking army heavily defeating the Irish under Uí Néill. Two years later the Vikings sailed into Lough Neagh and later set up bases at Annagassan and Dublin. Usually the Vikings departed after each raid, but in 841-42 they wintered at Dublin for the first time. This was to be the high point of Viking attacks at this time; post-850 their attention turned once again to England. However, many settled in Ireland, helping to establish trading links with Europe and, while never as dominant in Ireland as they were in England, the Vikings played a considerable role. Dublin was to become one of the major centers of the Viking world. A second wave of Viking attacks, in the second decade of the 10th century, saw the Irish heavily defeated at the Battle of Dublin in 919. It was to be another branch of the Vikings — the Normans (who had settled in northwest France) — that were to have a major impact on Ireland in the next Millennium.

## Arrival of the Normans

From the mid-10th century onward there was escalating internal strife in Ireland as the increasingly powerful provincial kings sought to establish greater power for themselves. One of these rulers was Brian Boru, who sought to challenge the powers of the Uí Néill clan. During the last two decades of the 10th century his power continued to grow until he had himself crowned King of Ireland in Dublin. Despite the title, he remained only a provincial warlord — but an influential one. He was killed during the Battle of Clontarf in 1014, when his forces proved victorious over the Viking settlers and their allies. Although this battle has been regarded as a triumph of the native Irish over the Viking invaders, in reality it was much more about the gradual emergence of a single Irish entity.

Across the Irish Sea, England was to be invaded, in 1066 by the Norman army, led by William the Conqueror. Following the famous Battle of Hastings at which the English king, Harold, was slain, Norman power gradually extended through all of England and the Norman realm was inextricably to link England with events in France and western Europe for the next 500 years. William's successors — Henry I and Henry II in particular — were to rule an Empire that incorporated much of France at a time when rising populations were bringing increasing threats of famine and disease.

The death of Brian Boru intensified the internal struggles for supremacy in Ireland and, increasingly, the warring factions started to look abroad for support. One of these warlords, Dermot MacMurrough, appealed to help from Henry II. This appeal led to the arrival of Anglo-

Norman forces in Ireland and the start of the process of colonization which set the pattern for Irish development through to Independence.

The factors behind Henry II's involvement were great. Dublin had been established already as a major trading center with links to England; more significantly, it was regarded by the church as subordinate to Canterbury. However, three synods held in Ireland — at Cashel (1101), Rath Breasail (1111) and Kells Mellifont (1152) — had established an independent Irish church hierarchy with Armagh at its apex. The clerics at Canterbury — fearing loss of income and prestige — had appealed to the Pope and, as a result of this, the Pope had invested Henry II with the right to rule Ireland. The result of this decree caused Henry to contemplate invasion as early as 1155/56, but in the event nothing happened for a decade.

In 1166, Dermot MacMurrough appealed for help. Using Bristol as a base, he raised an army which, from 1169 until his death in 1171, expanded his power base. Among his lieutenants was Richard fitz Gilbert de Clare, Earl of Pembroke, who was nicknamed "Strongbow." Following MacMurrough's death, Strongbow continued the military campaign despite injunctions to the contrary from Henry II. As a result of the disobedience of one of his feudal lords, Henry himself raided Ireland on October 17, 1171.

This was the point from which Anglo-Norman power started to be exerted strongly in Ireland. Inevitably, it was not a straightforward process, but inexorably the power of the native kings diminished as the power of the Norman lords increased. In 1175, for example, Rory O'Connor, King of Connacht, signed the Treaty of Windsor with Henry II. This treaty guaranteed O'Connor a certain amount of power outside those areas directly under Norman control, provided that he collected revenues due to Henry. However, as time passed, the treaty effectively became no more than allowing O'Connor to retain his increasingly diminished power in Connacht. Following the invasion of 1171, the Norman invaders from the late 12th century encouraged a policy of colonization. There were two major factors behind this. First, the division of Ireland into baronies with feudal land ownership was, in theory, an aid to centralized government and, secondly, it allowed for the movement of surplus population from England (and elsewhere) to settle. Ireland moved from a subsistence economy to one based on a series newly built market towns. It was at this time that Norman-French (for the aristocra-cy) and English (for the peasants) became the usual languages of those areas under Plantagenet control.

King John, who first visited Ireland in 1185, ruled from 1199 until 1216. Central power was strengthened, but only by slowing the pace of actual colonization. As administration improved and as laws were enacted, so the power of the monarch increased. Waterford and Cork came under the control of a single sheriff in 1207/08 and the forfeited lands of de Braose became the county of Munster. By the end of Edward I's reign, in 1307, Ireland had been divided into 12 counties, with only four "Liberties" remaining.

While it is theoretically attractive to regard this era as one which saw the power of the Anglo-Norman establishment rising while the importance of the native kings declined, this was not the case. The powerful Anglo-Norman lords were equally jealous of their power and prestige, and at this time the exercise of royal power was equally about the control of these barons as it was in terms of subjugating the native population. In England, the power of the barons had forced King John to sign the Magna Carta guaranteeing their rights in 1215; in Ireland, these same barons became powerful warlords in their own right.

Throughout the 13th century, increasing colonization brought greater competition, both between the Anglo-Norman barons and between the colonists and the native population. From the mid-13th century onwards Ireland was to see a number of revolts, but the march of the colonists was apparently inexorable. Yet while by 1300 the whole of Ireland was, nominally, under the control of the various barons or King Edward I, colonization in the west was subtly different to that of the east. There was not the surplus population to enable English-speaking settlers to move westwards, with the result that, in the west, the native population acquired feudal land tenure. This meant that the colonists' hold over the population was much weaker.

For Edward I and Edward II ownership of land was indivisible from the ability of that land to provide money and men to fight wars. England was at war with France and Scotland for much of the period, and the Irish exchequer was forced into near bankruptcy to help fund these campaigns. Not only this, but war spilled over from Scotland when, in May 1315, a Scottish army under the son of Robert the Bruce invaded Ulster. Although heavily defeated in October 1318 at the Battle of Faughart, this incursion helped to emphasize both the divisions between the barons and English king in Ireland and the weakness of the state. This frailty was compounded by a series of famines in the 1340s and by the onset of the Black Death in 1348-49; these events decimated the population, forcing many of the English settlers to return to England.

In the late 14th century some of the previously colonized lands were reoccupied by the native Irish; certain castles, such as Sligo and Ballymote, also passed to Irish possession. In order to counter the threat — which was exaggerated by the Anglo-Norman population — from the resurgent Irish kings and to retain control over the barons, a number of military operations were undertaken. In 1361-66 the English army under Prince Lionel of Clarence sought to restore colonial power. In 1369-72 and 1373-76 similar action was led by William of Windsor, while two campaigns in the last decade of the century, in 1394-95 and 1399, brought King Richard II to Ireland.

Ultimately, at this time, the question was one of overlordship. In the event it transpired that the ultimate victors were not the king nor the Irish leaders, but the Anglo-Norman magnates whose power was such that by the end of the 15th century, royal control in Ireland was effectively limited to the counties of Louth, Meath, Dublin and Wicklow. It was no coincidence that during the second half of the 15th century an earthen rampart — the Pale — came to be erected around the bulk of this area to defend it. Despite this, the 15th century was a period of some stability. There was a new feeling of Irish identity, reflected in the growth of traditional culture (such as the bards), much of which, paradoxically, was fostered by two of the great Anglo-Norman magnate families — the Butlers and the Geraldines.

## The 16th Century

At the end of the 15th century Ireland was both more prosperous and settled than it had been since the Anglo-Norman arrival. Yet, this prosperity was reflected in the building of castles, emphasizing the fact that the improved stability was relatively shallow. Much of this was the result of the power wielded, in particular, by the FitzGeralds, Earls of Kildare, and their families and it was the destruction of the Geraldine

power, along with the consequences of the Reformation, that were to mark Irish development over the next 100 years.

In 1494, an Englishman, Sir Edward Poynings, was appointed Lord Deputy of Ireland. This was a period when England itself was just emerging from the period of Civil War known as the Wars of the Roses. The Geraldines had been prominent in their support of the Yorkist pretender to the Throne — Edward Duke of York (later Edward IV) — and after the succession of the Henry VII, the first of the Tudor kings, in 1485, were also to support two of the colorful claimants to the throne — Perkin Warbeck and Lambert Simnel. Unable to rely on the backing of the Geraldines, Henry VII sent Poynings to Ireland. Among his various actions, he summoned a parliament to Drogheda which enacted Poynings Law. Effectively this stated that no parliament could be summoned in Ireland without the sanction of the King. Whilst it brought Ireland into line with England, the legislation had the immediate effect of weakening the power of the Lord Deputy.

For the population of the Pale, seeking a reduction of the power of the great barons and a restoration of closer links with the crown, the passing of Poynings Law was a triumph. However, by weakening the power of the Geraldines as Lords Deputy, the immense influence of the major barons — such as the Earls of Desmond in Munster, the de Burghs in Connacht and the FitzGeralds (Earls of Kildare) — was no longer in check. The result was factionalism, with each of the barons seeking to exercise greater control over those lords subservient to them. This made central government impossible.

It is important to recognize that, at this time, the English monarchs were perfectly happy to allow Ireland a considerable degree of latitude, provided that there was no overt threat to England. Of greater concern through much of the 16th century was continental Europe, particularly after the Reformation and the break of the English monarchy from Rome.

The Reformation was to have a further dramatic impact on Anglo-Irish relations. The Irish Catholic population — albeit willing to see reform of the church — never strayed from allegiance to Rome. One consequence of this was that positions in the state administration — which now required an acceptance of the monarch both as temporal and spiritual head — were no longer filled by those from Ireland. Increasingly, English-born Protestants filled these positions. Despite efforts to ensure

Catholic loyalty or conversion — such as Cromwell's actions in the 1640s — when James II, the first overtly Catholic monarch of Britain since the Reformation, attempted to regain the crown in 1689, he found a very sympathetic Catholic support in Ireland.

The first major rebellion of the 16th century occurred in 1534 when Thomas, Lord Offaly, a son of the 9th Earl of Kildare and a leading member of the FitzGerald family sought to restore the power of the FitzGerald family. Initially, this revolt was supported by many of the other leading Anglo-Norman families in Ireland. But when Henry VIII sent an army of 2,300 under Sir William Skeffington, Lord Offaly discovered that many of these so-called supporters were somewhat fickle and he was forced, as a result, to rely on support from the Gaelic Irish. Offaly's revolt failed and led to both the confiscation of FitzGerald family land and also the execution for treason of most male family members.

Following the defeat of the Offaly rebellion, the Irish parliament was called in 1536; this ratified in Ireland Henry VIII's separation from Rome and his remarriage. A further parliament in 1541 declared Henry VIII and his successors monarchs of Ireland. Despite Offaly's defeat and death, the FitzGerald name remained a potent force among the Gaelic Irish and the years subsequent to the defeat saw almost constant struggle between the Gaelic Irish and the residents of the Pale. The Anglo-Normans, supported by soldiers from England, gradually dispossessed the more radical Gaelic leaders, replacing them with English military rulers who exercised control over parcels of land from fortified garrisons.

However, the policy adopted by the English in the mid-16th century was never consistent; arguably, if the stricter policy had been more rigorously adhered to, then the major threats would have gradually been diminished. The real problem for the English was the cost of these major military actions. In principle, the costs incurred were to be recouped from profits generated from the lands confiscated. But, in practice, this rarely happened and — with the royal coffers already overstretched in England — there was an unwillingness to commit the Exchequer to greater expenditure in Ireland.

From 1556 until 1579, Ireland's history was dominated by the role of two governors, Thomas Earl of Sussex and Sir Henry Sidney, who followed widely differing policies. The former believed that stability would be achieved through military power and suppression of the Gaelic areas.

This policy was to lead to the creation of the first of the plantations (as colonization in Ireland became known) — that of Laois-Offaly — and to reform of the Anglo-Norman lands. But the plan also required a major military build-up, with consequent costs.

Sir Henry Sidney, first appointed in 1565, believed that an alternative approach, largely conciliatory but relying upon the transfer of lands from those opposed to the crown to those more sympathetic. The new communities thus established would be based around English, rather than Irish law. However, the reallocation of land led to problems. Many in England had long-standing claims to land in Ireland — often stretching back centuries. They felt that their rights should be restored. Many of these rights conflicted with the rights of the Old English establishment in Ireland which the governor could not afford to offend. There was also opposition which resulted in insurrection in Ireland. The policy was abandoned in the 1570s.

The most significant insurrection of this period was led by James Fitz Maurice FitzGerald. Having fled earlier to Europe, he landed in Ireland (in 1579) with a small army; decrying Elizabeth as a heretic — the first real occasion when religion as well as property rights became a major issue — FitzGerald gained support in Munster and from the Earl of Desmond and his brother. Elizabeth sent a force of 8,000 men under Arthur, Lord Grey de Wilton, who quickly defeated FitzGerald's force. The defeat led to swift retribution; many were executed and lands previously held by Desmond were declared forfeit. In order to strengthen English power, some 4,000 settlers (of a planned 20,000) were moved on to Desmond's estates and other Plantations were also developed.

The late 16th century was a period of considerable threat to Elizabeth. There were the various plots domestically which led ultimately to the execution of Mary Queen of Scots, while the Pope's Excommunication of the English queen made legitimate the schemes of the various Catholic monarchs of Europe to see Elizabeth overthrown. The most notable of these schemes was the planned invasion of England by the Spanish King (Philip II) — the Armada of 1588. In the event, the plan went sadly awry, when a combination of appalling weather and superb English seamanship saw the Spanish defeated. Following the Spanish defeat, many of the surviving ships were forced to sail round the British Isles *en route* back to Spain, with many foundering on Scotland's and Ireland's coasts.

In the period 1558–94 Sir William FitzWilliam was the governor of Ireland; he continued the policy of piecemeal colonization, extending it to Connacht and south Ulster. Ulster, at this time, was still dominated by the O'Neill family and Hugh O'Neill — who later became Earl of Tyrone in 1585 (thereby restoring the family title lost earlier in the century) — was a man of much ambition. Inevitably this led to conflict and, in 1601, the war was internationalized by the arrival of 4,000 Spanish troops sent to Kinsale (in Munster) by Philip II of Spain. Although approaching the end of her life, Elizabeth responded by sending 20,000 men. They soon defeated the uprising.

## Ireland Under the Stuarts

One of the consequences of O'Neill's rebellion was the realization among the English rulers that Catholic land ownership represented a potent threat to English hegemony. Ironically, this perception came at the same time as a new dynasty came to the throne of England — the Stuarts under James I, thereby uniting the crowns of England and Scotland — which was to be more sympathetic to the Catholic population than their Tudor predecessors.

Although James I, inheriting the crown shortly after O'Neill's defeat, was convinced of the correctness of a policy which saw many Catholic landowners dispossessed in favor of further Plantations (in the six counties of Ulster and elsewhere) with an immigrant population drawn now from both Scotland as well as England, both he and his son (Charles I) adopted policies towards the Catholics that saw many of the penal measures not fully implemented. Ireland at this time consisted of two distinct societies. These were not based on culture — Gaelic versus Old English (or Anglo-Norman) — but upon religion (Catholic versus Protestant), a division that had profound consequences on Irish history thereafter.

In the period prior to 1641, some 100,000 settlers, almost exclusively Protestant in religious belief, moved from the mainland to the new Plantations. The Plantations themselves were not wholly Protestant; a number of Catholics who had proved themselves sympathetic to the

crown were also granted (more limited) land rights. These became known as the "Servitors."

Charles I was married to a Catholic — Henrietta Maria — and was widely regarded by the increasingly powerful establishment in England as having pro-Catholic sympathies. The period between his accession (in 1625) and the start of the English Civil War (in 1642) was one of increasing conflict between the monarchy, with its adherents, and those who were opposed to it. It was inevitable that Ireland would be drawn into the conflict, particularly as, between 1635 and 1641, one of Charles's most loyal servants, Thomas Wentworth, later Earl of Strafford, was governor. Wentworth, just like the king in England and Scotland, became ever more unpopular largely as the result of the increasing demands for taxation. In England, this policy ultimately led to Charles being forced to summons Parliament. In Ireland, it led to a rising among many of the remaining Catholic landowners in Ulster.

The Ulster uprising of 1641 was a particularly bloody affair. Some 2,000 Protestants were massacred and many thousands of others were forced to flee. Support for the rising spread rapidly, with many of the old Irish establishment seeing the opportunity, once and for all, of eliminating English rule from Ireland. Given that English forces were otherwise engaged, it was not until August 1649 that Oliver Cromwell (one of the leaders of the Parliamentarian forces in the English Civil War and Lord Protector under the Commonwealth which replaced Charles I following the king's execution) was able to land in Ireland with a formidable — and highly trained — military force of some 20,000 men.

For the next three years Cromwell's army brought bloody retribution to Ireland. His policy was threefold: to eliminate military opponents; to remove opponents of English rule; and to encourage the Protestant religion. As part of this policy, wholesale changes of land ownership were planned and, in furtherance of this, a comprehensive survey of Ireland was undertaken by William Petty. His work ensured that, by the mid-17th century, Ireland was the best mapped of any European country. The proposed reallocation of land envisaged all land to the east of the Shannon being held by Protestant landowners while that west of the river would be in the hands of sympathetic Catholic owners.

The grand plan of Cromwell for the conversion of Ireland was, like many other proposals, never to be completed. The great experiment of Parliamentary rule in England was, by the late 1650s, drawing to a close

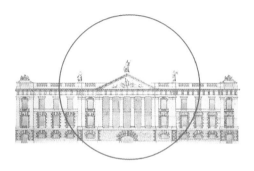

and it was clear that the Stuart monarchy would be reinstated. The actual restoration came in 1660 with the crowning of Charles II; Charles, like the later James II, was again more sympathetic to the Catholic population. The restoration also had one further consequence — royalist sympathizers, who had had their land confiscated, were to see their rights restored. In Ireland, however, restoration was limited; for the Catholic population, the only major change was that the anti-Catholic laws were less heavily enforced. Even so, Archbishop Oliver Plunkett of Armagh was still to be executed in 1681 following the Titus Oates plot.

In 1685, Charles II was replaced as monarch by his brother James, Duke of York. James, unlike Charles who, while sympathetic to the Catholic faith, was careful to ensure that the Protestant settlement was maintained, was much more overt in his pro-Catholic sympathies. As such, he alienated quickly the most influential politicians in England and compounded this with the appointment of Richard Talbot, later Earl of Tyrconnell, as Lord Lieutenant of Ireland. Talbot's policies, including the mobilization of a pro-Catholic army, simply exacerbated the concerns of the Protestants in both Ireland and England. These concerns led in 1688 to the overthrow of James II and his replacement by William of Orange (William III) and his wife Mary — the "Glorious Revolution" from which the British constitution (still unwritten at the end of the 20th century) derives.

In Ireland, the Revolution of 1688 led to war. James found a ready army in the Catholic population and received support from King Louis XIV of France. A number of Protestant towns, most notably Enniskillen and Londonderry, refused to surrender to James II and his Irish army, with the result that when William of Orange landed with his army in 1689 he found bridgeheads for his campaign against James. For Stuart power to survive, James needed to defeat William of Orange; in the event, a number of defeats including the Battle of the Boyne in July 1690 and the Battle of Aughrim in July 1691 saw the pro-Stuart forces defeated. With the Stuart demise, further restrictions on Catholic land ownership were imposed.

By the start of the 18th century, Ireland was effectively a British colony; although the majority of its 1.3 million citizens were Catholic, the rulers and the establishment were Protestant. The Catholic population represented about 75% of the total but owned only some 14% of the land. The next 100 years were to see Protestant power reinforced as anti-Catholic legislation was extended.

## Years Leading to the Act of Union

By 1800, the population of Ireland had risen to about five million. The century marked a period of considerable economic development, with both industry and agriculture expanding. In particular, the Irish textile industry — cotton, wool and linen — grew. This, in itself, was a source of tension with Britain, which sought to protect its domestic industry through restrictions on Irish commerce. The population growth — although not as great as it might have been without significant emigration to the British colonies in North America (from both Catholic and non-conformist populations) — was still such as to cause increasing tension by the end of the century, particularly amongst the disaffected.

The 18th century is commonly regarded as the era of Protestant supremacy in Ireland. Following the Stuart defeat, many additional legal restrictions were imposed. From the late 17th century onwards, there were barriers to Catholic education and even to the ownership of horses over a certain value. In 1729, the right of Catholic landowners to vote in elections was abolished. Despite this, many of the restrictions theoretically imposed on the Catholic majority were not rigorously enforced; indeed by the 1720s Catholic church building was allowed and by the 1750s Catholic seminaries were also open.

Reflecting the constitutional settlement in Britain after the Glorious Revolution, the Irish parliament sat regularly after 1690, but it was a parliament dominated by the Protestant landowning classes. There was nothing unique in this at the time; the parliament in London was equally the preserve of the landed classes (as indeed it would remain until the various Reform Acts of the mid-19th century). The actual rights of the Irish parliament were, however, constrained; two pieces of legislation — the infamous Poynings Act of the 16th century and the second passed by the British parliament in 1720 — effectively made the Irish parliament subordinate to British law; there was opposition to this from the so-called "Patriots." It would be wrong to see these as nascent freedom fighters. The Patriots were as much a part of the Protestant establishment as the rest of the Irish parliamentarians — their concern was equally to ensure the survival of the Protestant control but rather from a standpoint of greater power in Dublin. It should be noted that non-conformists were also heavily discriminated against.

The major political players in Ireland at this time were known as "Undertakers;" this was the result of the fact that these factions undertook to manage affairs on behalf of London in exchange for preferment to the major jobs in government. Just as politics was divided in London between the Whigs and the Tories, so the "Undertakers" in Ireland supported different factions. Increasingly, however, by the middle of the century, the monarch's representative in Ireland, now known as the Viceroy, was based at Dublin Castle more often, thereby allowing for the creation of a "Castle Party" which dealt directly with the major figures in Ireland.

Despite the increasing wealth and population, Ireland was still not securely governed. A standing army was retained, particularly to counter the still perceived threat from the Stuarts. This became a serious danger in both 1715 and 1745 when the Old and New Pretenders attempted to regain the crown — and towards the end of the century the increasing pressure on land led to rural violence. This violence was contemporaneous with the rise of radicalism and revolution in both North America — particularly in the events leading to the Declaration of Independence in 1776 and the subsequent war against the British authorities — and in France — where the revolution brought both the downfall in 1789 (and later execution) of Louis XVI and also war against the British.

Patriot leaders like Henry Grattan and Henry Flood were vociferous in their demands for greater independence, albeit still under the crown. Further instability was caused by the foundation of the United Irishmen, initially in Belfast and later in Dublin, whose aspirations were heavily influenced by the radicals in France who believed in the creation of an Irish republic. The Dublin branch was suppressed by the authorities in 1794, and was forced to convert itself into a secret society. British policy was complex; on the one hand various restrictions — such as the 1720 Act and Poynings Law — were either repealed or amended to appease the Patriots, while on the other many of the anti-Catholic measures were also lifted, which had the effect of antagonizing the Protestant hierarchy. In 1795, Earl FitzWilliam became Viceroy; his policies of increasing Catholic emancipation alienated yet further the Protestant power with the result that he was repudiated by the government in London and quickly replaced. It was the perceived threat to the Protestant hegemony that led, in the mid-1790s, to the creation of the first lodges of the Orange Order. This institution, which remains active today, became one of the bedrocks of the pro-Union establishment.

One of the leaders of the United Irishmen was Theobald Wolfe Tone and it was he, following a period of exile in France, who assisted the French to invade Ireland at Bantry Bay in December 1796. This major force was, however, largely dispersed by adverse weather conditions and the invasion failed. This was one of a number of attempted incursions and rebellions. In May 1798, a rising began in Leinster and on the 30th of that month Wexford was captured by rebels. Their success was, however, limited and they suffered two major defeats: New Ross on June 5, and Vinegar Hill on June 21. On August 22, 1798, a further French force under General Humber landed at Killala; a government army was defeated at "Races of Castlebar" on August 27, but Humbert was forced to surrender at Ballinamuck on September 8. Following a further French raid on Lough Swilly, Tone was arrested on November 3, 1798 and he committed suicide in prison on November 19.

The continuing threat of violence and of insurrection was one factor in the initial proposals by the then British Prime Minster, William Pitt the Younger, for an Act of Union between Ireland and Britain. These proposals were first made in January 1799, and were to be linked with greater Catholic emancipation. The Act of Union was passed on August 1, 1800, and took effect from January 1, 1801. It is from that date that the Union Flag started to incorporate the red cross of St Patrick. The second strand of Pitt's policy — that of Catholic emancipation — was rejected by the crown the following month, with the result that Pitt resigned. The failure to achieve emancipation at this time was seen among many in Ireland as a further British betrayal of trust.

## Period of the Union

The Act of Union brought significant changes over time. For example, the Irish were now entitled to send 100 MPs to the Parliament at Westminster and a Free Trade area now encompassed the whole of the British Isles. However, the status of the Catholic majority as second-class

citizens was not changed initially; reform only took place gradually — Catholic Emancipation affecting the whole of the British Isles (and not just Ireland) was enacted in 1829 — and almost from the start of the period of Union there was opposition. Partly this was due to the continued presence the trappings of colonialism — such as the presence of the Viceroy in Dublin Castle — along with the persistent stationing of troops in barracks.

In 1803, Robert Emmet led a rebellion; this was shortlived and Emmet was executed later that year. In 1823, the Catholic Association was formed; this was part of the growing politicization of the Catholic population in Ireland. Following rejection by the House of Lords of a bill allowing for Catholic emancipation in 1825, the electors of Waterford discarded, in 1826, Lord George Beresford in an election for that constituency. At a time when constituencies were largely controlled by the powerful landowners, this was indicative that traditional power was in decline. This was further exemplified two years later when Daniel O'Connell was elected MP for Clare. O'Connell, one of the early leaders of the Home Rule movement was by inclination a pacifist who sought, via his links with the Whig government in London, to achieve a greater measure of independence. Through the funding of his movement — the so-called "Catholic Rent" — increasing numbers of the disenfranchised became involved in the political process.

O'Connell's influence, however, began to wane from 1841, when the Tory Sir Robert Peel became Prime Minister, and his desire to operate within the law — exemplified by his cancellation of a banned meeting at Clontarf in 1843 — led him gradually to be marginalized by the increasingly radical movement. O'Connell himself was to be convicted of "conspiracy" in 1844, although this was later overturned on appeal and in 1846 he was to split with the Young Ireland movement — one of the new radical bodies — over the use of force.

In 1841, the population census recorded the Irish population as over eight million; a decade later it had dropped to six million. From the mid-1840s onwards the Irish question was dominated by famine. The rapid expansion of the Irish population during the first half of the 19th century was not unique — similar growth had occurred in Britain. But whereas in Britain much of the population rise had been accommodated in the increasingly important industrial cities — Manchester and Birmingham, for example — in Ireland industrialization was slower and traditional land ownership patterns meant an increasing fragmentation of farms. The Famine, caused by the failure of the staple potato harvest, was to affect Ireland severely; some three million people emigrated — the vast bulk to the USA — over this period although emigration itself was not new.

The decade after the Famine was to witness a new radicalism among those seeking greater independence. In 1859, James Stephens founded in the USA the Fenian Brotherhood; he had the previous year founded the Irish Republication (or Revolutionary) Brotherhood in Dublin. Fenianism spread to Ireland in 1865. The name "Fenian" was derived from the Fianna, legendary Irish heroes. In North America, Fenians undertook a raid across the Canadian border in May 1866. In February 1867, Irish Fenians attempted to seize Chester and also, in December 1867, tried to blow up Clerkenwell Gaol, in which 12 were killed. In early March 1867, there were attempted risings led by Fenians in Munster and around Dublin. These, however, came to nought.

One factor in the failure of the Fenian movement was that Ireland, in the 1860s and 1870s, was undergoing a period of prosperity and stability. However, it was stability based on the fact that the population was continuing to shrink as emigration continued unabated. With the onset of a recession in North America in the early 1870s, this avenue was no longer an option and increasingly disaffected young people were forced to remain in Ireland with its very limited opportunities. Another factor in the prosperity was that the emigrant Irish population regularly sent large amounts of money back to Ireland.

From 1870, constitutional moves in support of Home Rule gained pace. In 1870, Isaac Butt founded the Home Government Association and three years later Charles Stuart Parnell created the Home Rule League; emphasizing the fact that the religious divide played only a minor role at this stage, both Butt and Parnell were Protestants. It was also in 1873 that the Irish Republican Brotherhood rejected violence as a means of achieving Home Rule, placing their support behind Parnell. In the event, however, violence was never far from the surface and the IRB's endorsement was withdrawn in 1876. In 1879 the foundation of the Irish National Land League brought the issue of land ownership to the fore again; despite Land Acts in 1870 and again in 1881, the issue of tenant rights caused an increase in tension, with numerous murders and evictions. This tension was reflected, on May 6, 1882, by the Phoenix Park Murders in Dublin, when Lord Frederick Cavendish and T. H. Burke — the Chief Secretary and Under-Secretary — were assassinated. Their deaths were not a direct result of the land issue but a reflection of a growing anarchy within Ireland.

Parnell, who had been jailed in 1881–82 and released following the Kilmainham Treaty, condemned the Phoenix Park Murders and later won a libel action against the *Times* newspaper which had, on the basis of forged documents, claimed that Parnell was implicated in the deaths. In 1885 Parnell's political party gained 80 percent of the Irish seats in Parliament, thereby holding the balance of power. Realizing that the only way that he could retain political power was through an alliance with the Parnellites, the Liberal Prime Minister, William Ewart Gladstone, became a convert to Home Rule. In April 1886, Gladstone introduced the first of his Home Rule bills but this was defeated. The result of the bill was a serious split within the Liberal Party and also the emergence of militant Unionism following a speech in Belfast by Lord Randolph Churchill.

By 1890, Parnell's coalition — which had united the Liberals under Gladstone, the Catholic Church and the Home Rule movement — was beginning to fall apart. One factor in this was that he was cited as co-respondent in a divorce case brought by Captain William O'Shea. Gladstone, a man of strong moral beliefs, refused to deal further with Parnell and, by the latter's death in October 1891, Gladstone had abandoned him. A second Home Rule bill was presented in 1893; although this passed the House of Commons, it was to fail in the House of Lords.

Contemporaneously with the rise of Home Rule on the political agenda at Westminster, the threat to the Union began to galvanize anti-Home Rule groups in Ireland. Primarily Protestant in origin, these new groups owed less to the landowning classes of the Ascendancy than to the new Protestant working class of Belfast and Ulster. A mark of the sectarian intimidation was the reduction in the numbers of Catholics employed in the engineering workshops of Belfast. The new militantism was demonstrated through groups such as the Irish Unionist Alliance of 1891 and the Ulster Unionist Council of 1905. There were efforts to follow a middle line — such as Robert Lindsay Crawford's Independent Orange Order of 1903 — but these were destined to failure as the Home Rule crisis developed prior to the outbreak of World War I.

In 1910, a new Liberal government came to power under Herbert Asquith. Just as with Gladstone in 1885, this new administration needed to rely on support from the Irish Parliamentary Party for power and, once again, Home Rule was on the political agenda. One consequence of the 1910 election was the passing of the 1911 Parliament Act. This severely constrained the rights of the House of Lords to reject legislation passed by the House of Commons — as had happened in 1893 — and thus made it more likely that a Home Rule bill would be enacted.

The tensions within Ireland at this time were great. In Ulster, 200,000 men — three-quarters of all male Protestants in Ulster over the age of 15 — signed the Solemn League and Covenant on September 28, 1912. In January 1913, the Ulster Volunteer Force was established; it soon boasted a membership of some 90,000 and had access to some 30,000 illegal arms. The major figure in the pro-Unionist campaign at this time was Sir Edward Carson, the founder of the Ulster Unionist Council, who drafted a proposed constitution for a partitioned Ireland; the proposal for partition was, however, rejected by the British government in early 1912.

As a counter to the UVF, the pro-Home Rule movement established, with John Redmond as its president, the Irish (National) Volunteers. Again, this organization had access to illicit weapons and, as the Home Rule bill gradually went through Parliament — it was eventually to pass in 1914 but was not enacted — it appeared increasingly likely that conflict would break out between these two armed militia. An attempt at compromise — the Buckingham Palace conference — ended in failure.

## Easter Rising and its Aftermath

That civil war did not occur in 1914 was the result of hostilities breaking out elsewhere. Following the assassination of Archduke Franz Ferdinand in Sarajevo, the European military alliances found themselves at loggerheads — on August 4, 1914 Britain declared war on Germany. The reaction in Ireland to the outbreak of war was interesting. In September 1914, Redmond announced that members of the Irish National Volunteers would serve against Germany, but this precipitated a split between the INV. In May 1915, the Military Committee of the IRB Supreme Council was instituted and in December of the same year the Military Council of the IRB was formed; the latter represented the signatories of the 1916 proclamation.

In January 1916, the IRB decided on an early rebellion. On April 3, 1916, the INV was ordered to prepare for action. On April 21, Sir Roger

Casement arrived from Germany; two days earlier a shipment of arms from Germany, on board the *Aud*, was seized. On April 23, 1916, Easter Sunday, the Military Council of the IRB confirms rebellion. Early on April 24, INV members captured buildings in central Dublin. The rebellion lasted only a few days, collapsing on April 29; 14 of the leaders were executed for treason early in May. The Easter Rising was led by P. H. Pearse of the IRB and by James Connolly of Sinn Féin. Sinn Féin ("Ourselves Alone") had been founded in 1902 by Arthur Griffith (1871–1922); it was not to achieve any real significance until the Easter Rising. In the election of 1918, Sinn Féin — led at this stage by Eamonn de Valera — gained 73 out of the 105 Irish parliamentary seats. Sir Roger Casement was captured in June 1916; sent to London for trial, he was executed for treason on August 3, 1916.

One consequence of the Easter Rising was that, in June 1916, the Ulster Unionist Council agreed to Home Rule provided that the six counties of the future Northern Ireland were excluded. In place of Home Rule, however, the Irish Convention was established on May 16, 1917; the convention continued until April 5, 1918, but achieved little.

In January 1919, violence returned to Ireland with the Soloheadberg ambush, when six members of the INV murdered two policemen. On April 1, the first meeting of the unofficial Irish parliament — the Dáil Éireann — met in the Mansion House in Dublin; de Valera was elected president. Later in the month, a general strike broke out in Limerick. Following the increasing breakdown in law and order, the British government acted. Sinn Féin and other organizations were suppressed in areas of strife, such as Tipperary, while de Valera headed for the USA, where he remained until mid-1920. In September 1919, the Dáil Éireann was declared illegal. In January 1920, the first of the Black & Tans — additional recruits for the Royal Irish Constabulary, so called because they were forced to wear non-standard khaki and dark green uniforms — were recruited. The Black & Tans became a highly controversial body when, faced by terrorist activity, they responded with atrocities of their own. The most infamous Black & Tan incidents included the occasion when two Irishmen were killed at Balbriggan in September 1920, and another when one of the main streets in Cork was set on fire in December 1920, destroying several of the city's major public buildings.

In May 1920, the railwaymen began a strike, refusing to carry troops on trains. This severely hampered the ability of the authorities to exercise law and order. In July, there were serious sectarian riots in Belfast; these were repeated in August when 30 were killed. In order to cope with the threat of increased guerrilla warfare, an "Auxiliary" — nicknamed the "Auxies" — force was raised. In an effort to regularize the situation, the British government enacted a Restoration of Order Act on August 9, but the situation deteriorated, with atrocity being met with reprisal. On one occasion the IRA murdered 11 British officers on November 21, 1920 and, in response, the Black & Tans killed 12 football supporters later the same day. This day became known as "Bloody Sunday." Martial Law was imposed in December 1920 in Cork, Kerry, Tipperary and Limerick as the authorities sought to regain the initiative.

On December 23, 1920 the British government enacted the Government of Ireland Act. This allowed for the setting up of a parliament and administration in the six counties of the future Northern Ireland and also — but never fulfilled — a similar structure for the south. The violence continued into 1921. On May 25, for example, the Customs House in Dublin was burnt down. On June 22, King George V opened the first session of the new Ulster parliament. On July 9, 1921, there came a cessation of hostilities with a cease-fire between the IRA and the British forces. The scene was now set for the negotiation of a treaty which was to shape the future destiny of Ireland.

The conference to determine the treaty first met in London on October 11, 1921 and a formal Anglo-Irish Treaty was signed on December 6. Following the signature, the treaty was debated in the Dáil Éireann starting on December 14, and formally approved on January 7, 1922. On January 9, 1922, Arthur Griffith, the founder of Sinn Féin in 1906 and the head of the Irish delegation to the London Conference, was elected President of the Dáil where he succeeded Eamonn de Valera. Even at the London Conference, however, there had been splits among the Irish delegation, with figures like Erskine Childers coming out against the settlement. The scene was set for Civil War.

## Civil War

The Irish Free State was created following a treaty signed on December 6, 1921 by Lloyd George and by Michael Collins and Arthur Griffith representing the Irish Free State. The treaty gave Ireland dominion status. However, it was denounced by sections within the

Republican movement, with opposition being led by Eamonn de Valera. Despite this opposition, the new constitution was adopted in October 1922 and the Irish Free State was proclaimed in December 1922.

The Civil War was, arguably, more traumatic for Ireland than the struggle against the British; it led to a split within the Republican movement with old comrades being forced into violent opposition and many of the old certainties no longer applicable. The anti-treaty forces undertook a campaign of assassination of leading supporters of the treaty — such as Michael Collins, commander-in-chief of the Free State army, who was killed in County Cork on August 22, 1922 — while the Free State forces were forced to maintain law and order. In total some 73 anti-treaty activists were executed by the authorities in the Free State between November 17, 1922 and May 2, 1923. These included Erskine Childers (the author best known for *The Riddle of the Sands*, one of the first books ever published on espionage, which warned of the German threat to Europe prior to World War I) and many leaders of the Republican movement, such as Liam Mellows and Rory O'Connor, both of whom were executed on December 8, 1922. Another architect of the treaty, Arthur Griffith, President of the Dáil in 1922, was also not to survive the Civil War; he died of a cerebral hemorrhage later in 1922.

The origins of the Civil War violence dated back to the occupation of the Four Courts building in Dublin by Irregulars opposed to the treaty in April 1922. For a couple of months there was a stand-off, but on June 28, 1922 — following an electoral triumph for pro-treaty candidates in a General Election on June 16 — pro-treaty forces attacked the Four Courts to remove the Irregulars; violence returned to Dublin and the Civil War ended. By the time that Eamonn de Valera led the anti-treaty forces to surrender their arms in May 1923, some 800 Free State soldiers had been killed. The casualties on the anti-treaty side were even greater.

## *Republic After the Civil War*

Following the treaty establishing the Irish Free State (Soarstát Éireann) and the Civil War in the south between the pro and anti-Treaty factions, the Free State continued initially as a nation within the British Empire with the monarch remaining as head of state.

From the Civil War, two political parties emerged — Fine Gael (Family of the Irish) and Fianna Fáil (Comrades of Destiny) — both of which continue to this day and which have dominated Irish politics since partition. Traditionally the former was pro-Treaty and the latter anti. The Irish constitution, however, retained clauses which assert sovereignty over the six counties that formed Northern Ireland; it was only in the referendum held after the Good Friday Agreement in 1998 that these clauses were finally consigned to history.

In December 1931, the Statute of Westminster gave effective legislative freedom to the Dominions — including Ireland — and in 1932, an electoral victory by Fianna Fáil (which was pro-Republican) led to an increased disregard of the formal ties with Britain (and a disastrous tariff war with its neighbor to the east which lasted until 1936).

The next stage in the evolution of Ireland as a sovereign nation followed the abdication of King Edward VIII in 1936 and the succession of his brother King George VI. On December 29, 1937, a new constitution came into force, which declared Ireland to be "a sovereign, independent, democratic state" under the name of Eire. Although the constitution provided for the election of a president, it was not until April 1949 that Ireland became a republic — the Republic of Ireland (Poblacht na Eireann) — and left the British Commonwealth. Recognition of Irish independence came from the British Parliament the following month.

During the period of World War II, Ireland remained neutral. Northern Ireland was, as part of the United Kingdom, heavily involved in hostilities. US forces were also based in there once the USA entered the war. There were suspicions that Eamonn de Valera, the then Prime Minister of Eire, had pro-German feelings, and there were Allied plans to invade Eire in the event of a German occupation. As a result of the 1921 Treaty, Britain retained access to harbors at Cork, Bantry Bay and Lough Swilly, and these were important in the protection of the transatlantic convoys that ensured Britain's survival after the fall of France in 1940.

In the 30 years after the end of World War II the traditional pattern of Ireland continued. There was little or no population growth as emigration — either to Britain or to North America — continued, with many of the brightest young people being forced to leave in search of opportunities which the still agrarian-based Irish economy was unable to provide. The major turning point came on January 1, 1973 when, like the United Kingdom, Ireland became a member of what was then called the European Economic Community, although the unemployment level was to peak at 20 percent in 1987. Today known as the European Union and with a single currency under development (of which the Republic, unlike the United Kingdom, has chosen to become a founder member), the former EEC has proved to be a great facilitator of economic development in Ireland. Through the various Regional Development Funds, the Republic of Ireland has, over recent years, experienced considerable economic development, with growth higher than any other state in the union. As a result, the population decline of previous decades has ceased, with many newly qualified graduates now electing to remain at home and the traditional "brain drain" being reversed. Prosperity means that the republic is no longer the poor relation of northern Europe.

## Northern Ireland After Partition

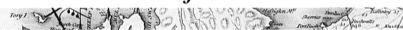

Following the Government of Ireland Act of December 1920 a separate parliament was established for the six counties that were to form Northern Ireland. Proposals during the 1920s for the redrawing of the borders between Northern Ireland and the Irish Free State, which would have removed some of the anomalies, were stillborn.

Northern Ireland, with a population of between 1.2 and 1.5 million during the period (roughly half of that south of the border), had a Protestant and Unionist majority, although there was a sizeable minority of Catholic pro-Nationalists included. The nature of the constitution and the Unionist control of the Stormont Parliament in Belfast, however, meant that the rights of this minority were frustrated. Between 1920 and 1969 there were periods of anti-British activity, much of it sponsored by the Irish Republican Army, most notably between 1956 and 1962, after which the campaign was called off.

In an era when minority rights were being widely recognized elsewhere in the world, it was inevitable that the minority in Ireland would seek to gain a greater voice. In January 1967, the new Northern Ireland Civil Rights Association was founded; in the following year a number of protest marches were organized which led to clashes with the authorities. The situation deteriorated yet further two years later and British troops were sent into the Province in August, initially with the intention of providing protection for the Catholic minority. However, the situation continued to deteriorate and, from the early 1970s, the Provisional IRA — created following a split within the organization in January 1970 — commenced the struggle against the authorities. The British government suspended the Stormont Parliament, having recognized that this was part of the problem, and instituted Direct Rule.

Over the next 25 years, violence was never far from the scene in Northern Ireland. Attempts at a peaceful settlement — such as power sharing in the mid-1970s, the Women's Peace Movement of 1976 (which resulted in Betty Williams and Mairead Corrigan receiving the Nobel Prize for Peace), and the Hillsborough Agreement in 1985 — failed to stem the tide of bloodshed as a result of the inability of the various factions to agree a settlement. The atrocities perpetrated by both sides have been well covered elsewhere.

However, as the new Millennium approaches there are hopeful signs that a new accommodation between the two traditions within Ulster may be forthcoming. Although the initial August 1994 cease-fire declared by the Provisional IRA proved shortlived, it was to be reinstated in 1997 and all-party talks under the auspices of the new Labour government led to the Good Friday Agreement of 1998.

The agreement, with its all-Ireland institutions and devolved administration in Ulster, has seen elections and has resulted in John Hulme and David Trimble receiving the 1998 Nobel Prize for Peace. For the first time in more than a generation, there are real hopes of a lasting peace.

Renegades on both sides — such as the perpetrators of the Omagh bombing (ironically the single worst atrocity in terms of loss of life of the whole period of the "Troubles") — do exist but they are being increasingly marginalized. The vast majority of Irish people, both north and south of the border, hope that in the future Ireland will be known simply for its booming economy, its superb landscape and its remarkable heritage — and not for terrorism and violence.

## *Reasons for Cartography*

At a most basic level maps were required to record the physical presence of land and of physical features. In particular, information regarding secure havens was required and, as knowledge increased, so these charts developed into maritime charts detailing safe channels, expected water depths, hazards to navigation and so on. It is important to remember that for much of the period covered by these maps all trade was sea-borne and the vulnerable ships of the period were at the mercy of the harsh climate often to be encountered.

Out of discovery came possession and many of the maps produced from the mid-16th century were designed to show land ownership. On a global scale, these maps could illustrate the distribution of land between the great nation states, often as a result of a settlement after a war. At a more local level, the maps could illustrate the ownership of parcels of land that had been divided between individual landowners. While the more global representation of the region was suspect, certainly in the early days, the smaller the areas covered the greater the accuracy. There had been a long tradition of detailed estate maps in Europe, in particular among the abbeys and major land owners, and mapping of a small locality was, therefore, a skill widely practiced.

Finally, from possession comes conflict. The military were among the most important map makers, with the skills and resources to undertake precise surveys. It is no accident that the United Kingdom's primary mapping agency has the name Ordnance Survey as it grew out of a department of the military.

## *Development of Cartography*

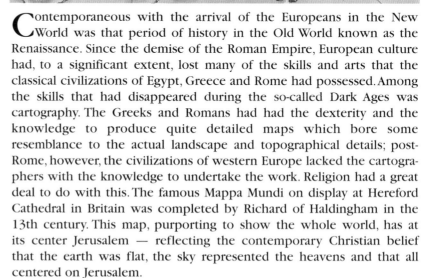

Contemporaneous with the arrival of the Europeans in the New World was that period of history in the Old World known as the Renaissance. Since the demise of the Roman Empire, European culture had, to a significant extent, lost many of the skills and arts that the classical civilizations of Egypt, Greece and Rome had possessed. Among the skills that had disappeared during the so-called Dark Ages was cartography. The Greeks and Romans had had the dexterity and the knowledge to produce quite detailed maps which bore some resemblance to the actual landscape and topographical details; post-Rome, however, the civilizations of western Europe lacked the cartographers with the knowledge to undertake the work. Religion had a great deal to do with this. The famous Mappa Mundi on display at Hereford Cathedral in Britain was completed by Richard of Haldingham in the 13th century. This map, purporting to show the whole world, has at its center Jerusalem — reflecting the contemporary Christian belief that the earth was flat, the sky represented the heavens and that all centered on Jerusalem.

The Renaissance — or "rebirth" — was a period of flowering in the arts and in literature. It was an era when scientific discoveries were being made and when mankind's knowledge of the world was increasing. Exploration, both by land and by sea, had expanded awareness of the earth and had undermined fatally the existing tenets. During the later Middle Ages, there was an increasing skill in cartography, just as there was in art, and this was initially reflected in local or district maps. These small scale maps were often the result of property disputes or of the major landowners, often the church, delineating their property.

At the start of the 15th century, the production of these local maps grew dramatically. To this was added the production in 1406 of a map produced by Ptolemy, a late Roman cartographer, of a map (of the then known world) drawn in a style similar to that which we would recognize today. This map was widely circulated and in 1475 the first printed version appeared. With the arrival of printed maps, the skills of the cartographer — which previously had been limited to only a handful of people, many of them monks in the major monasteries — became more widely dispersed.

Just as the knowledge of cartography was increasing, so too were the skills associated with surveying. Although still rudimentary by modern day standards, the principle of constructing maps by actual measurement was growing in importance. Units of measurement may have varied from country to country, even district to district, but the moment that maps became scaled so they became more useful to, for example, property owners and to mariners. The skills associated with the construction of detailed maps were also enhanced during the 16th century by the discovery of triangulation, the art by which the relative positions of places could be determined through the use of a precisely measured base line and detailed use of angles.

Many of the early cartographers were not specifically trained. Some — like Leonardo da Vinci — were artists and scientists interested in expanding human knowledge; others came from more mundane backgrounds. The great British cartographer John Speed, of the early 17th century, was a tailor by profession. A figure like Speed was able to develop as a cartographer, without ever having visited the regions that he portrayed, for two reasons. Firstly, he was able to copy the work of earlier cartographers as the concept of copyright as we know it today did not exist. Secondly, this information could only come to him through the increasing availability of detailed prints produced by craftsman, many of whom came from the Low Countries (Belgium and Holland). This latter point is of note; these craftsman-printers were producing printing plates in languages that they were not well versed in. It was inevitable that place names would be mis-spelt and these errors would be perpetuated by those using the printed maps as sources for newer publications.

By the start of the 16th century, the skills required to produce detailed scale maps were in place. Many of the earliest drawn were produced by the military — for either offensive or defensive reasons — and the military were, as the maps in this book show, to maintain an important role in cartography right through to the modern age. Many of the scale maps produced still retain elements of the older tradition of pictorial representation. To cartographers in the Renaissance, and to those working today, the pictorial representation of buildings and other facilities helps to codify. The pictorial representations that are visible in many of the maps included in this selection have three effective roles: to decorate; to provide a useful symbol (for a church or house, for example); and, to form a foundation for other information.

## About the Maps

All the maps illustrated in this book have been drawn from the large collection held by the Public Record Office at Kew in west London. This is the major holding of all public documents in the United Kingdom. The maps are derived from a number of government departments and reflect the interests and concerns at the time they were compiled. Given England's interests in Ireland from the mid-16th century onwards — from when the first of these dates — many of the maps held by the PRO are unique and normally accessible only to researchers. There is added interest in many of these earlier maps because of the annotations made upon them by Elizabethan ministers such as Sir William Cecil, help to emphasize that these were not only a record of the physical shape of Ireland, but also an essential part of the maintenance of English rule.

## Place Names

Most place names in Ireland can be written in either an English or Gaelic form. This book uses the form of the name that is best known. This means, for example, that Dublin is used rather than Baile Atha Cliath or Dubhlinn, although the Gaelic names will be discussed and their origins explored where appropriate. It should also be noted that a number of place names, of which the most conspicuous contemporary example is Londonderry or Derry, have a political connotation. This book does not seek to make political points about the use of names; the names cited in the captions for each map are those which were in use by the cartographers at the time. Thus, for example, Kingstown is now better known as Dun Laoghaire (translated as Leary's Fort) and Queenstown as Cobh. Two counties have also changed their names in the Republic — King's County and Queen's County becoming Offaly and Laois respectively. This list is not meant to be a comprehensive listing of all names, but will help to indicate the rich heritage demonstrated by place names throughout the island of Ireland.

| ENGLISH SPELLING | GAELIC NAME | MEANING OF GAELIC NAME |
|---|---|---|
| Ardmore | Ard Mor | Big Hill |
| Armagh | Ard Macha | Macha's Hill |
| Athlone | Ath Luain | Luan's Ford |
| Ballinrobe | Baile an Rodbha | Town of the River Robe |
| Bantry | Beanntraighe | Beanne's Descendants |
| Belfast | Beal Feirste | Sandy Ford |
| Bray | Bri Cualann | Cuala's Hill |
| Bundoran | Bun Dobhrain | Mouth of the Dobhran |
| Carlow | Ceatharlach | Fourfold Lake |
| Cashel | Caisel Mumhan | Stone Fort of Munster |
| Cavan | An Cabhan | Hollow Place |
| Clonakilty | Clanna Chaoilte | O'Keelty's Clan |
| Clonmel | Clua in Meala | Honey Meadow |
| Cork | Corcaigh | Marshy Place |
| Derry | Doire | Oak Wood |
| Donegal | Dún na nGall | Fortress of the Foreigners |
| Drogheda | Droichead Atha | Bridge over the Ford |
| DublinBaile | Atha Cliath | Town of the Hurdle Ford |
| Dublin | Dubhlinn | Dark Pool |
| Dundalk | Dún Dealgan | Delga's Fort |
| Kildare | Cill Dara | Church of the Oak |
| Kilkenny | Cill Chainnigh | Canice's Church |
| Killarney | Cill Airne | Church of the Sloe |
| (Kingstown) | Dún Laoghaire | Leary's Fort |
| Kinsale | Ceann Saille | Tide Head |
| Letterkenny | Leitir Ceanainn | O'Cannons' Hillside |
| Limerick | Luimneach | Barren Spot |
| Lismore | Lios Mor Muchuda | Mochuda's Great Hill Fort |
| Londonderry (Derry) | Doire | Oak Wood |
| Macroom | Maghcromtha | Sloping Valley |
| Monaghan | Muineachain | Little Hills |
| Mullingar | Muileann Caerr | Carr's Mill |
| Navan An | Uaimh | The Cave |
| New Ross | Ros Mhic Treoin | Wood of Treann's Son |
| Roscommon | Ros Comain | Coman's Wood |
| Sligo | Sligeach | River with Many Shells |
| Tipperary | Tiobard Arann | Well of Arann |

| ENGLISH SPELLING | GAELIC NAME | MEANING OF GAELIC NAME |
|---|---|---|
| Tralee | Traigh Li | Bay of the River Lee |
| Tuam | Tuaim | Burial Place |
| Waterford | Port Lairge | Lairge's Landing Place |
| Westport | Cathair na Mart | Stone Fort of the Cattle |
| Wexford | Loch Garman | Garman's Loch |
| Wicklow | Cill Mhantain | St Mantan's Church |

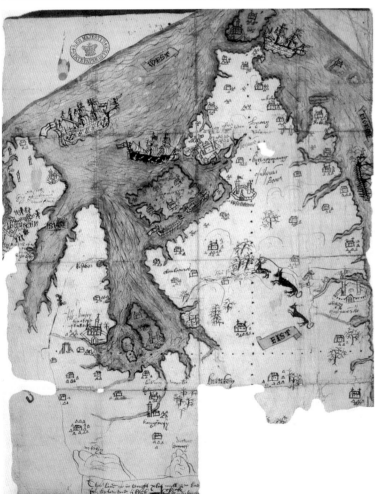

## Ireland c.1558

**Left:** This is a rough sketch map, drawn originally in pencil and later inked over, which portrays the whole of Ireland. There are additional annotations by Sir William Cecil. It was in 1558 that Elizabeth succeeded her half-sister, Mary, as Queen of England, re-establishing the Protestant succession to the throne. At this time the English governor of Ireland — from 1556 to 1564 — was Thomas Radcliffe, Earl of Sussex. He undertook both military campaigns to reduce the threat to English hegemony in Ireland and also inaugurated the policy of colonization — "Plantation" — which sought to strengthen England's power through the transfer of land from Irish land owners to English settlers.

## Bantry Bay c.1558

**Below Left:** Showing Bantry Bay and the country round, in counties Cork and Kerry, along with Kemare River and Dunmannus Bay, this manuscript map shows the various fortifications in this area at the start of the reign of Queen Elizabeth. Bantry Bay is one of the most beautiful locations in Ireland. The climate, influenced by the Gulf Stream, is temperate with a profusion of palm trees and other plants not normally associated with the British Isles. As a safe natural harbor, Bantry Bay has acted as a base for invasion; on two occasions — in 1689 and 1796 — when French forces attempted to land here in support of anti-English armies. Between Bantry Bay and, to the south, Dunmannus Bay lies the long promontory known today as the Sheep's Head Peninsula. Reflecting the usefulness of the natural harbor, Bantry Bay is today partly occupied by a major oil terminal.

## Ireland c.1567

**Right:** This is one of the oldest maps of Ireland held by the Public Record Office that can be precisely dated. The legend — in Latin — reads *Hibernia: Insula non procul ab Anglia vulgare Hirlandi vocata*, which can be translated as "Hibernia: an island not far from England, in the common tongue called Ireland." The map was drawn by John Goghe with annotations by Sir William Cecil (later Lord Burghley and one of Queen Elizabeth's most influential ministers). The map, which shows the whole island of Ireland and its relationship with England, Scotland and Wales, is aligned with the east-west axis forming the vertical. Pictograms delineate the various towns and cities, along with woodland and hills. With its identification of family names, it is contemporaneous with the adoption by the English authorities of a policy of colonization. This process, the Plantation, sought to transfer land ownership from the Irish native population to English settlers in the belief that the arrival of large numbers of colonists would increase the loyalty of Ireland to the English crown. It was a means by which, in theory, the power of the major Irish landowners would be reduced.

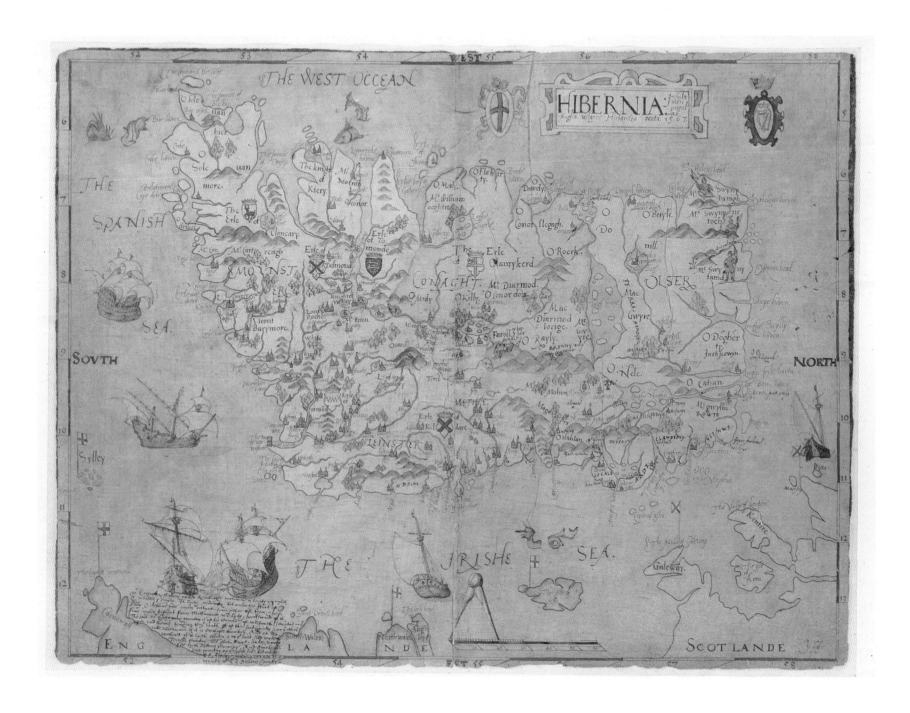

23

# Belfast Lough c.1569

**Below:** Ascribed to Robert Lythe, this parchment map is possibly a copy of a map originally produced by Christopher Saxton after Michael Fitzwilliams. It shows Belfast Lough, with Belfast itself, Carrickfergus, Larne Lough, Island Magee, Bangor, etc. Although Belfast possessed a castle from the 12th century, the city's prominence did not really develop until after the Act of Union in 1800 and the impact of the Industrial Revolution. Carrickfergus Castle was a major military fortification; built originally at the end of the 12th century it was one of the centres of Anglo-Norman power in Ireland. Held for a period by the Scots in the 14th century, its fortifications were strengthened in the 16th century as a result of the threat of Irish rebellion. For a period in 1760, during the Seven Years War, Carrickfergus Castle was held by the French.

# County Down c.1570

**Right:** This is a map, probably drawn by Robert Lythe, showing the coast of County Down from Lough Strangford to Carlingford. The scale is about two miles to one inch. In the top right, information regarding the total acreage is given in a cartouche. This map is contemporaneous with the first private colonization of Ulster and portrays the landscape before large numbers of English and Scottish settlers arrived.

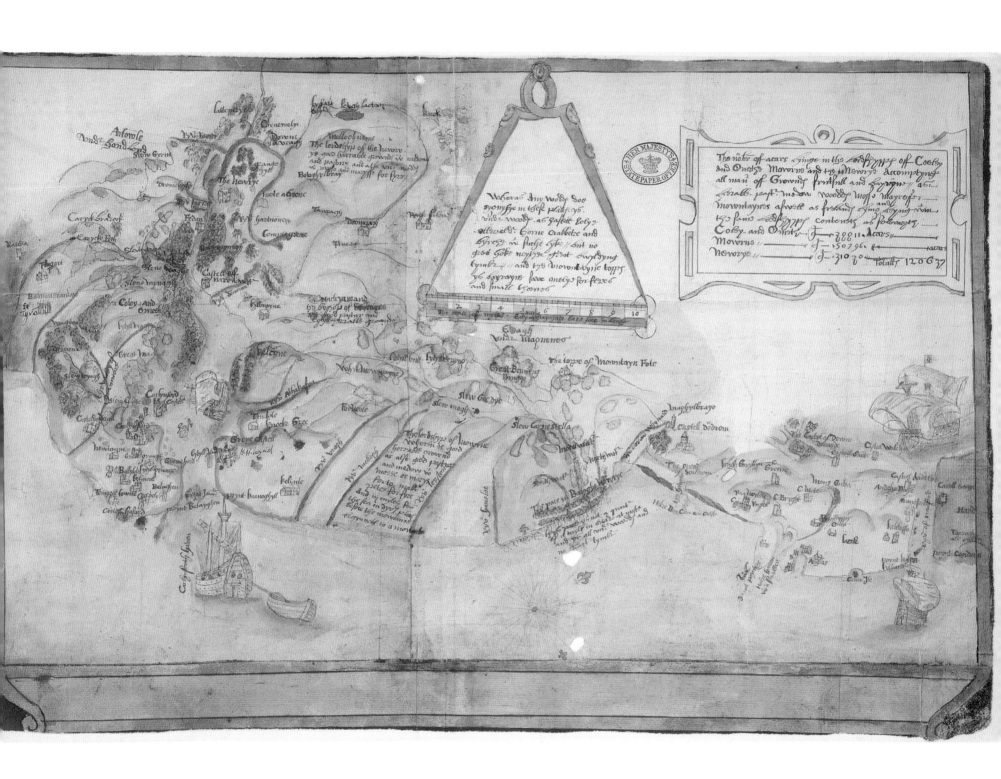

25

## Newry c.1570

**Right:** Possibly drawn by R. Lythe, this map shows the various buildings in the town of Newry — castle and church included — in perspective. It was drawn to a scale of about 80 feet to one inch. Newry is situated in County Down; the river — with a ford indicated — marks the boundary between the counties of Armagh and Down, both of which today form part of the modern Northern Ireland. Note that the castle is described as "new" and that the town itself if provided with walls and a moat. The map predates the establishment from 1605 of the Plantation in County Down.

## Newry c.1570

**Below:** This, and the next illustration, shows the castle at Newry during the reign of Queen Elizabeth I. Possibly drawn by R. Lythe, it shows the front elevation of the castle and was drawn to a scale of eight feet to one inch. Newry's origins date back to the foundation of a Cistercian monastery in 1144, but the town's real importance came from its strategic position controlling the so-called "Gap of the North." This was the narrow point at the head of Carlingford Lough which provided the most direct access into Ulster from the south. Over the years a number of fortified structures were built to control the route; of these none survive today. The castle as illustrated here is more akin to a fortified manor house than the traditional castle of the Middle Ages. By the 16th century structures such as this were becoming more domestic in style and across the Irish Sea in England, the relative peace of the period was to see the trend towards the construction of the great stately homes, which abandoned overt defensive qualities in favor of architectural splendor.

## Newry c.1570

**Right:** This is a second illustration of the now lost castle at Newry dating from the early years of the reign of Queen Elizabeth. It shows well the arrangement of the four floors with which the building was provided and the location of the spiral staircase in the projecting tower.

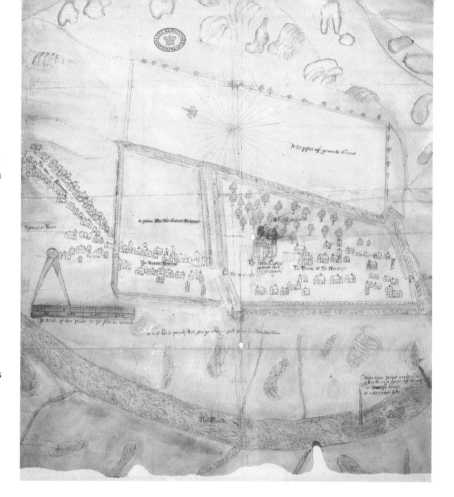

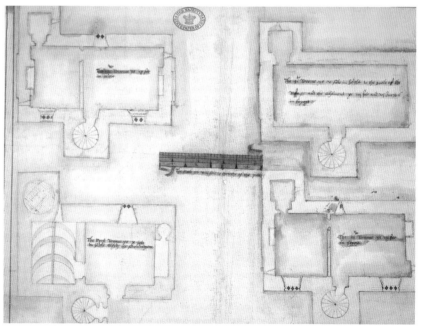

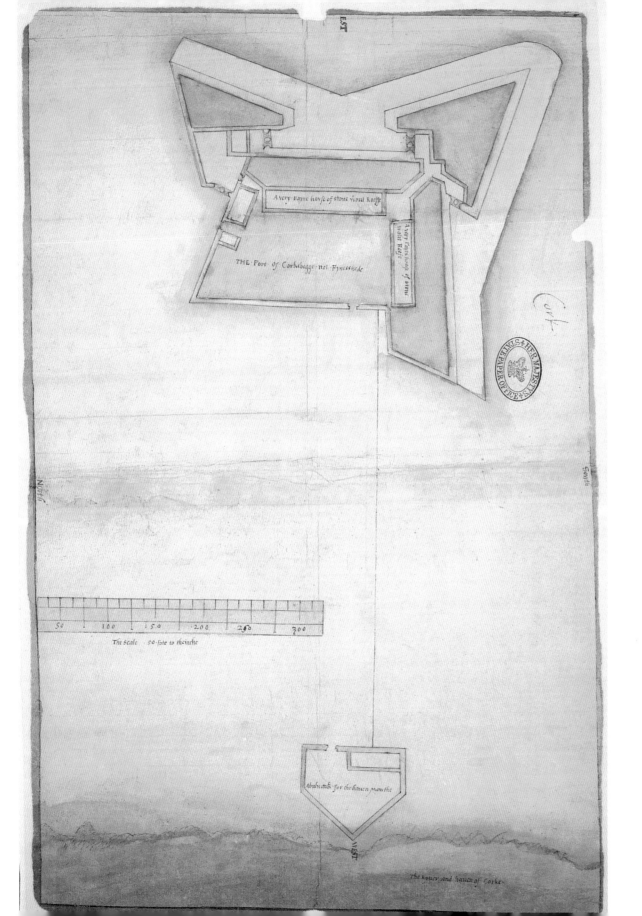

Within the map:

EST

A very fayre house of stone without Roofe

A very fayre house of stone without Roofe

THE Fort of Corkebegge not Fynesshede

Cork

HER MAJESTIES PAPER OFFICE

North

South

50    100    150    200    250    300

The scale · 50 fote to the inche

Abulwark for the haven mowthe

WEST

The Ryver and haven of Corke

## Corkbeg Fort c.1571

**Left:** Described as "The fort of Corkbegge not fynesshede," this map was drawn to a scale of 50 feet to one inch by Robert Lythe. In addition to the fort, the map also shows a bulwark at the haven mouth. This was one of the fortifications planned or constructed for the defense of Cork; at this time (from 1571 to 1575) Sir William Fitzwilliam was Governor of Ireland. This was a critical period for the English as, in 1570, Queen Elizabeth had been excommunicated by the Pope. Until this point, Elizabeth had sought to maintain a balance between the Catholic and Reformist elements within England. However, following Excommunication, Catholics no longer, in theory, owed allegiance to Elizabeth and, from 1570 onwards, English authorities moved much more overtly into an anti-Papist stance. At a time when monarchs were still believed to rule by Divine Right, Excommunication was a direct threat to Elizabeth's power base. Ireland, with its Catholic majority, was perceived by the English as a potential ally for the strong Catholic monarchies of France and Spain, both eager — for different reasons — to see Elizabeth's demise.

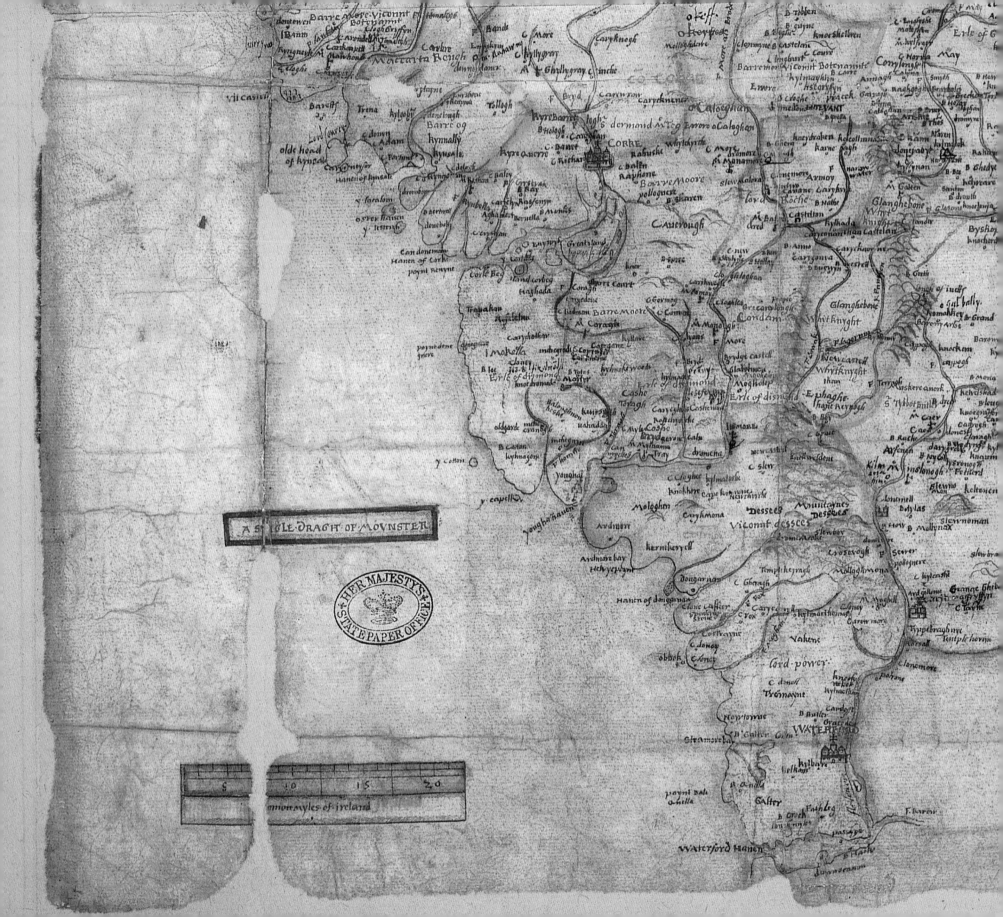

A SINGLE DRAGHT OF MOVNSTER

HER MAJESTYS STATE PAPER OFFICE

## Munster c.1572

**Left:** Possibly drawn by Robert Lythe, this is a manuscript map of Munster, the most southwesterly Province of Ireland. Apart from illustrating the topographical features — coastline, rivers, etc — and the settlements, the map is also of interest in that it shows the names of the Irish nobility and chieftains. As with a number of other maps derived from the Elizabethan State papers, it has also been annotated by Sir William Cecil. Cecil was one of the most important and influential of all Elizabeth's ministers. At a time when the English crown was under threat both domestically and internationally as a result of the monarch's rejection of Catholicism, Cecil, among his many other duties, ran a network of spies and informers to ensure that the crown and its ministers were well informed about treasonable plots.

## Castlemaine c.1572

**Below:** County Kerry is one of the six counties which form the Province of Munster. This pen and ink drawing records the siege of Castlemaine by Sir John Perot (or Perrott), Lord President of Munster, in 1572. It shows the castle spanning the River Main, Perot's camp, other encampments as well as cannon firing at the fortified bridge. Warfare at this time, as throughout history, depended upon the holding of strategic river crossings and numerous fortified structures of this nature were built. The River Maine is one of the tributaries that flow into Dingle Bay; Castlemaine is situated just to the south of Tralee and the Dingle peninsula. The engagement recorded here was part of a campaign waged by the Lord President against rebels in Munster; a similar campaign was wrought by Sir Edward Fitton in Connacht at the same time.

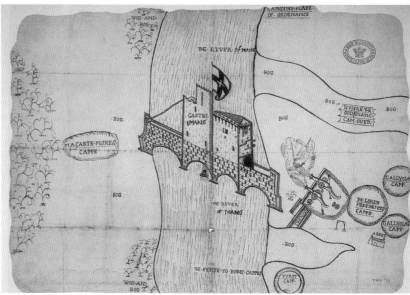

## Wicklow 1579

**Left:** Portraying the newly made counties of Wicklow and Ferns, which comprised parts of the modern counties of Wexford, Wicklow, Carlow and Dublin, this map, like many others from the Elizabethan state papers, has been annotated by Lord Burghley. Drawn to a scale of about two miles to one inch, it indicates the various baronies in the area. The region covered is that to the south of Dublin and the map is aligned with west to the top and east, with the coastline, to the bottom. Topographically, Wicklow is dominated by the 40-mile long range of the Wicklow Mountains; these mountains run north to south through the county and provided a barrier to military action as there were only two passes from east to west through them. Following the revolt of 1798, the authorities constructed a military road through the district in order to improve communications.

## Munster c.1580

**Left:** This map shows the Province of Munster — the most southwesterly of the Irish Provinces — with the exception of County Clare (to the north of Limerick). Place names, rivers, forests and towns are clearly portrayed, the latter being illustrated by buildings in elevation. The scale is 13 Irish miles to an inch. Note that the cardinal points are again inserted in the border, but that the orientation of the map is not the north to south that 20th century maps would conventionally adopt. Among places clearly evident are Limerick, Cork and Waterford. Cork straddles the River Lee and its history began in the 7th century with the foundation of the monastery dedicated to St Finbar. Limerick's origins date back to the arrival of the Vikings in the 9th century, when the area was used by them as a base from which they could pillage the country. The castle and bridge were constructed from 1210 on the orders of King John. Waterford was, like Limerick, founded by the Vikings (in 853) as Vadreford. Again like Limerick, it was one of the strongpoints of English power in Ireland.

## Ulster c.1580

**Right:** This manuscript map shows the nine counties of the Province of Ulster. Oriented with west to the top and east to the bottom, it is drawn to a scale of about seven miles to one inch. Places named include Belfast and Derry. About a decade prior to the drafting of this map, the first private-venture colonists started to settle in Ulster, a process which was to continue through much of the 1570s. Although the colonization scheme was supposed to assist the cementing of English power in Ulster, this was not to be immediately successful and in the last decade of the 16th century and the first of the 17th, Ulster was at the forefront of rebellion to English rule.

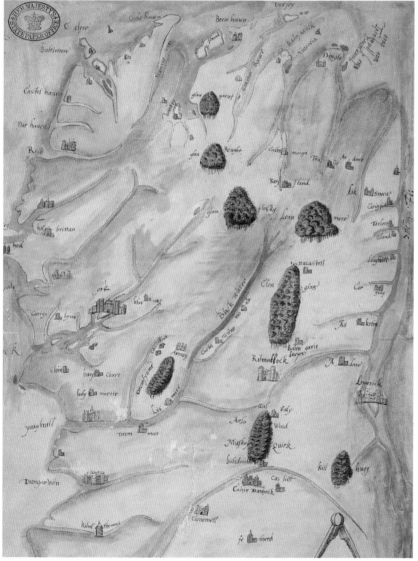

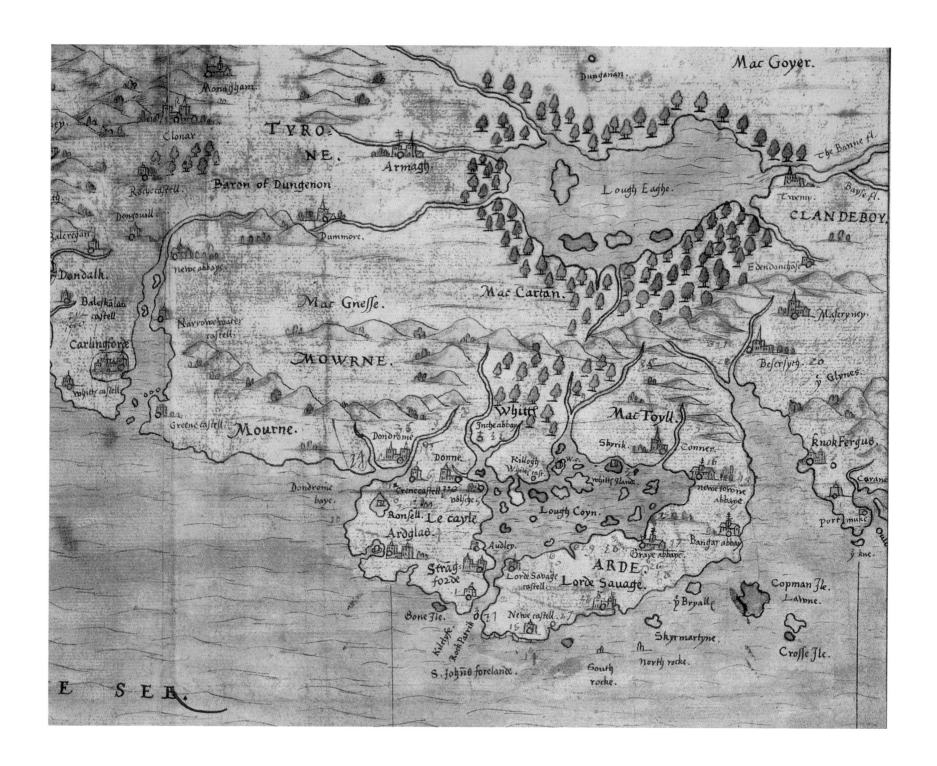

Mac Goyer.

Dunganan.

TYRO-
NE.
Armagh

Monaghan.

Clonar

Rochecastell.
Baron of Dungenon
Dongouill.

Dummore.

Lough Eaghe.

The Banne fl.

Twemy.

Bayse fl.

CLANDEBOY.

Dondalk.

Baleskalan
castell

Carlingforde

whith castell

Newe abbaye.

Mac Gnesse.

Narrowewater
castell.

Mac Cartan.

Edendonchase.

Maseryney.

MOWRNE.

Beserspth. 20
ÿ Glynes.

Greene castell
Mourne.

Dondrome

Dondrome
baye.

Whitte

Inche abbay

Donne

Killogh
Whitt tast.
W.c.

whith glana

Skyrik.

Mac Toyll.

Conner.

knok Fergus.

Corane

newe torone
abbaye

port muke

Crencastell
wolsche.

Ronsell.
Ardglas.

Le cayle

Audley.

Lough Coyn.

Graye abbaye.

Bangar abbay.

Strag-
forde

Bone Jle.

Kilbyse.
Rock Darth

Newe castell. 27

Lorde Sauage
castell

ARDE.
Lorde Sauage.

ÿ Brpalle

Skyrmartyne.
South
rocke.
North rocke.

Copman Jle.
Lavone.

Crosse Jle.

S. Johns forelance.

E SEA.

32

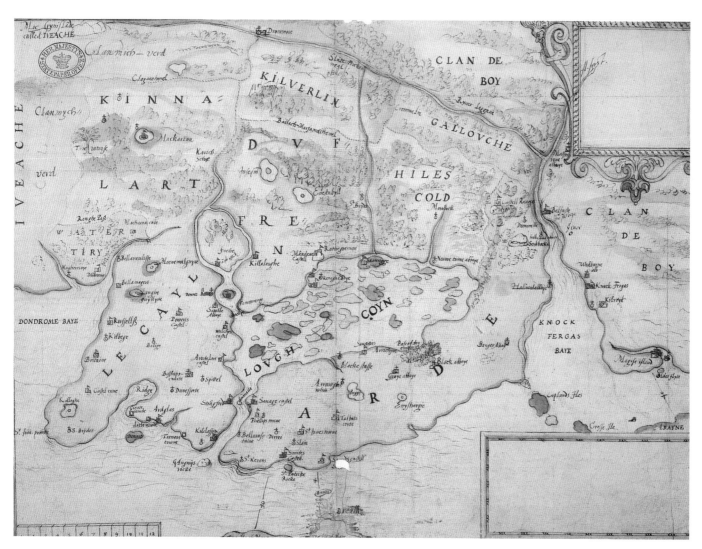

## Ireland c.1580

**Left:** Showing the coastline from Dundalk to Carrickfergus (Knokfergus), this colored manuscript map is scaled at about 6.5 miles to one inch. It is part of a larger map showing the coastline from Dublin northwards. Principal place names and abbeys are identified, although the spellings may not be as readily identifiable to a modern audience. Note that the distances between Ardglas and the Isle of Man (90 miles) and between Oulderflete (effectively modern Whitehead) is 28 miles from Galloway in Scotland; this is not quite the closest point between Britain and Ireland — the Mull of Kintyre is slightly nearer.

## County Down c.1580

**Above:** A further map oriented with west at the top and north at the right this illustrates part of County Down — one of the nine counties of the original Province of Ulster and one of the six that form the current Province of Northern Ireland. Among places identified are Ardglass (Ardglas) and Belfast (Belfaste). The stretch of water described as "Lough Coyn" is known today as Strangford Lough, whilst "Knock Fergas Baye" is Belfast Lough. This region of County Down is the most easterly point of the island of Ireland. On the extreme east (ie towards the bottom of the map) can be seen the west coast of the Isle of Man in the middle of the Irish Sea; although land-based mapping had, by the 16th century, started to reflect distances with some approximation of accuracy, the inter-relationship between different islands by water still represented difficulties.

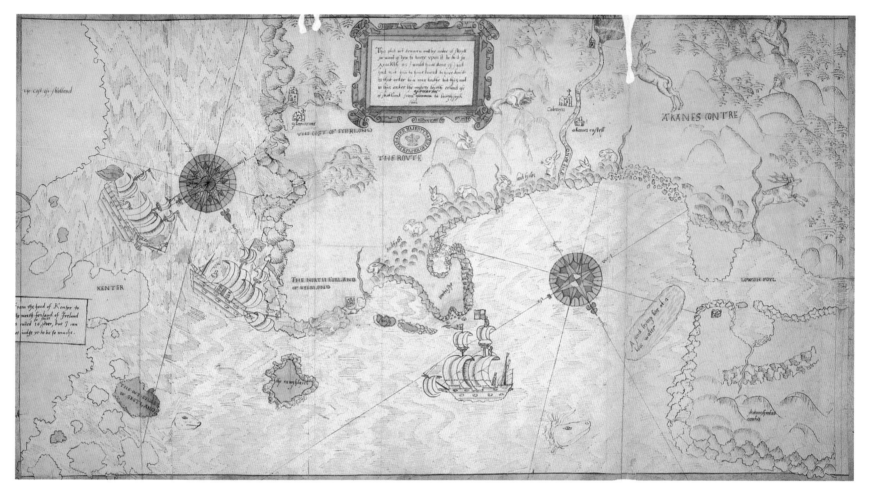

## Antrim c.1580

**Above:** Antrim is one of the original nine counties of Ulster and is today one of the six which make up the Province of Northern Ireland. Colrayn (Coleraine) and Lowgh Foyl (Lough Foyle — the approach to Londonderry) are identified. The map shows the proximity to the coast of Skotland (Scotland) and the Kenter (Kintyre). The north coast of Antrim, to the east of Coleraine, is the Giant's Causeway — one of the most popular tourist destinations in Ireland today.

## Portrush c.1580

**Above Right:** This map shows the promontory of Portrush in Antrim. North is towards the base of the map. The scale is about 200 yards to one inch. Note the sailing ship, with its oars, flying the flag of St George; this was (and is) the flag of England — the familiar Union Flag (including the crosses of St Andrew and St Patrick) is the flag of the United Kingdom of Great Britain and Northern Ireland and is much later in date. The area illustrated here is the Giant's Causeway. This is a natural rock formation comprising some 40,000 separate basalt columns. In legend, the Giant's Causeway was the result of the work of Finn McCool. Falling in love with a giantess from the island of Staffa in the Hebrides, McCool decided to construct a pathway to allow her to get to Ulster.

34

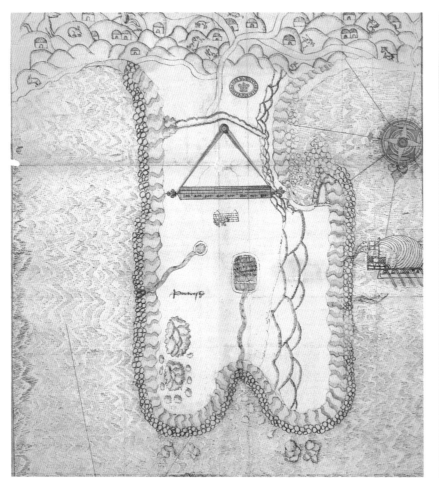

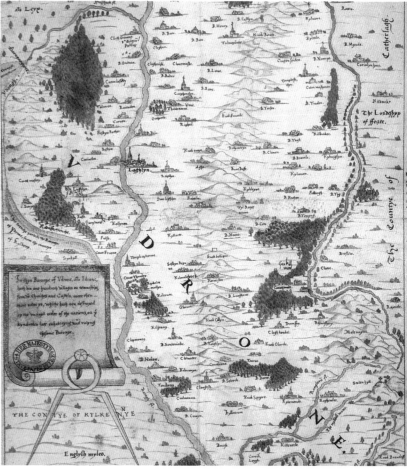

# Idrone c.1580

**Above Right and Right (details):** Drawn at a scale of about 0.8 miles per inch, this map shows the hills in relief, rivers, woodland, places named and buildings delineated in perspective. The Barony of Idrone was situated in County Carlow, one of the smaller counties that formed the Province of Leinster. Carlow is situated southwest of Dublin. Amongst places identified are "Catherlagh" (Carlow) and "Laghlyn" (Leighlinbridge). Carlow was an important settlement situated on the border of the English "Pale" — the Anglo-Norman area round Dublin — and the rest of Ireland. Its military importance was recognized in 1361 with the construction of a rampart; thereafter it became a focus of much military activity. The last engagement fought at Carlow occurred in 1798, during the French Wars, when some 640 Irish rebels were killed. The castle remains are now a National Monument. Leighlinbridge marks one of the crossings over the River Barrow and, like Carlow, its castle — Black Castle — is today a National Monument. The structure which survives is a product of a 16th century rebuilding of a castle constructed in 1180 to protect the crossing, emphasizing how far Carlow was a border area at that time.

THE DESCRIPTION of the Baronye of Vdrone, in y Countye of Catherlagh in the Realme of Irelande.

In thys Baronye of Vdrone, als Idrone, hath ben one hundreth villages or towneships, fom w Churches and Castels, more then — there nowe ys, whiche hath ben destroyed by the vnciuyll order of the nations, or y kyndredes late enhabityng and rulyng thesame Baronye.

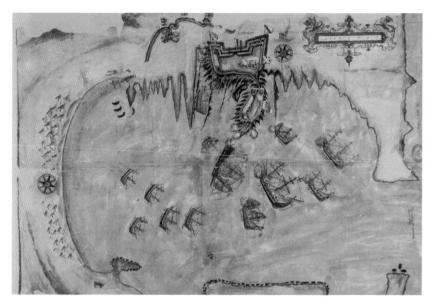

## Smerwick Harbor 1580

**Left:** This dramatic scene shows the siege of the *Castello del Oro* by ships of Elizabeth's Navy. Among vessels named is the *Revenge*, one of the most famous of all Elizabethan warships. The *Revenge* was the first of the major men-of-war — or "galleons" — constructed. Launched in 1575, she was 92 feet long and 32 feet wide; displacing some 450 tons, she was equipped with 50 guns and had a crew of 250 men. Regarded by Sir Francis Drake as the most perfect warship, *Revenge* was to last until 1591 when, under the command of Sir Richard Grenville, she was sunk in an engagement against the Spanish. The battle recorded in this map, which was drawn by William Winter, shows the English forces attacking the European ones which had landed in Munster in support of James Fitz Maurice Fitzgerald. Following the defeat of the rebellion, the victorious English put the leaders of the plot to the sword and devastated much of the area. The lands of the Earl of Desmond and other supporters of the rebellion were declared forfeit to the crown and some 20,000 English settlers were encouraged to migrate to the area.

## Roscommon 1581

**Left:** Roscommon is one of the five counties of the Province of Connacht. This map, probably drawn by Sir Nicholas Malby in July 1581, shows the town and castle of Roscommon, the county town, clearly delineating the defenses and the area within the ramparts destined for the construction of buildings. An abbey was founded at Roscommon by Felim O'Conor, King of Connacht, in 1253, although there is evidence that an earlier abbey existed. The abbey, along with the contemporaneous castle, are now both National Monuments.

## County Mayo 1585

**Right, Above and Below:** Mayo is one of the five counties which makes up the Province of Connacht in the northwest of Ireland (the others are Sligo, Leitrim, Roscommon and Galway). Although this map is identifiably the county, it is aligned east to west on the vertical rather than the more usual north to south. The Atlantic Ocean is, therefore towards the top of the map and the north point faces to the right. Clearly identifiable are The Mullet peninsula, Achill (Akill) Island, Lough Maske (Loghe Maske) and Lough Corrib (Loghe Corby). The map delineates the various topographical features, including the Nephin Beg range of hills running westwards towards Achill Island. With an area of some 55 square miles, Achill is the largest of Ireland's offshore islands. Situated on Achill Island are the ruins of Carrickkildavnet Castle; in the 16th century, shortly after the date of this map, Carrickkildavnet belonged to Grace O'Malley (c.1530–1603), the "pirate queen" of Irish legend and song. She was the only child and heir of the head of the O'Malley clan; her father lived by the sea — fishing and piracy — and, following a period of marriage, she was to follow in his footsteps in 1566 as the first woman to head the clan. A pragmatist, she traveled to London in 1593 to plead for the release of her son and paid homage to Queen Elizabeth I. Her men and ships terrorized much of western Ireland and the adjacent parts of the Atlantic Ocean. They were ruthless in the extreme; on one occasion, following the murder of her then lover, she had the entire family of the perpetrator killed.

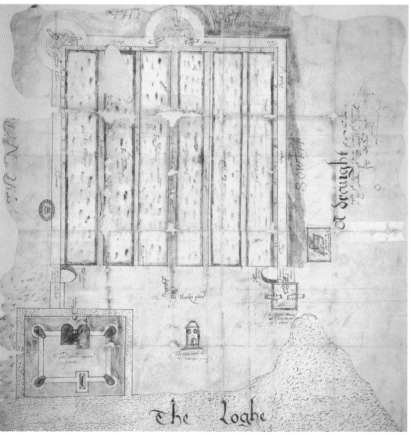

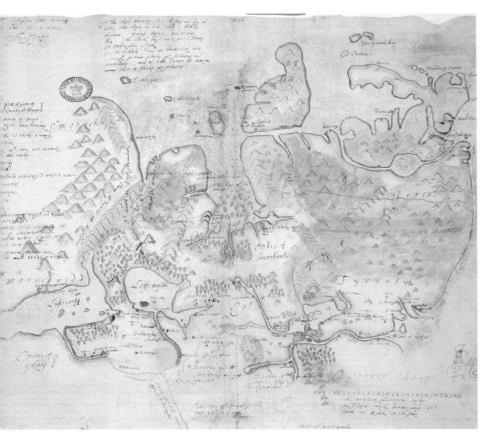

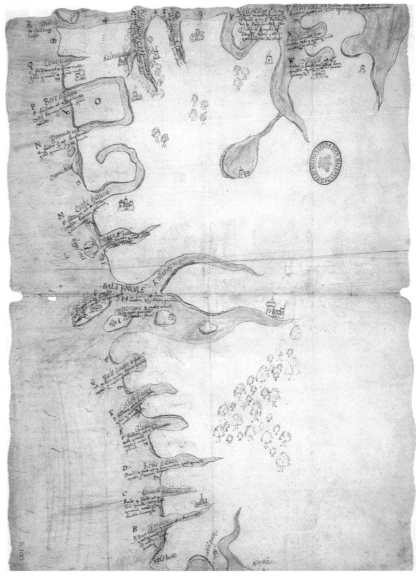

## Cork and Kerry 1587

**Above:** This manuscript map shows the coastline from Kinsale to Dingle. Featured prominently are soundings at low water, holding ground and havens; the havens are distinguished by a separate letter — from "A" to "Y." The map helps to bring home the fact that the sea (and water generally) was the only real means of communication and that much of the mapping of this period — indeed right up to the present day — is designed to ensure safe navigation. Safety at sea, particularly for the small wooden sailing boats of the period, was critical and knowledge of the safe havens was essential.

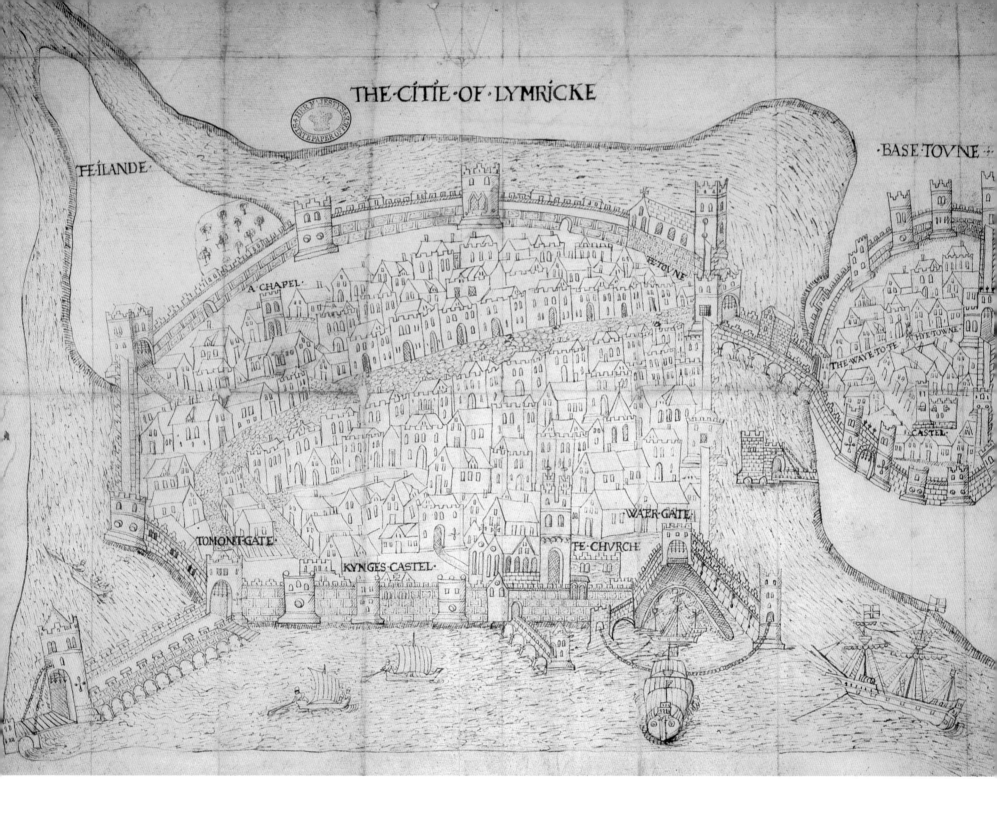

THE·CITIE·OF·LYMRICKE

BASE·TOVNE

FE·ILANDE·

HER·MAJESTY·STATE·PAPER·OFFICE

A·CHAPEL·

FE·TOVNE

THE·WAYE·TO·TE·HYE·TOVNE

CASTEL·

WAER·GATE

TOMONT·GATE·

FE·CHVRCH·

KYNGES·CASTEL·

38

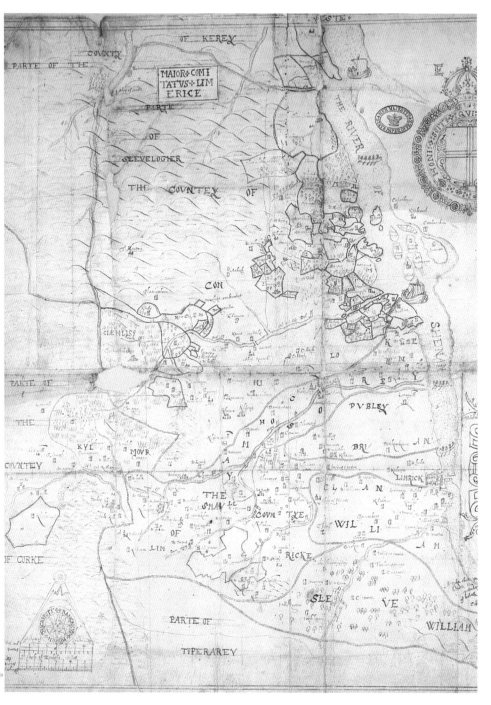

## Limerick 1587

**Far Left:** Limerick, in County Limerick in the Province of Munster, is today one of the most important cities in the Irish Republic. This map shows in perspective the city towards the end of the reign of Queen Elizabeth and illustrates well the town's strategic importance on the River Shannon. At the center of the drawing is the area known as English Town today; the area is surrounded by walls and by the natural defenses offered by the Abbey River and by the River Shannon. A gated bridge, with drawbridge, provides a well defended crossing of the River Shannon, while the King's Castle is the structure built on the orders of King John in the early 13th century. The castle is now a National Monument. Also visible is the church (now cathedral) of St Mary. Limerick was provided with its own harbor area; this was accessed through the Watergate. Across the Abbey River is the area then known as "Base Town," which is today called Irish Town.

## Limerick 1587

**Left and Below:** With an axis that runs from west at the top to east at the bottom, this map shows County Limerick and its relationship with the neighboring counties, including Cork and Tipperary. It delineates the subdivisions of the county and the land held directly by Queen Elizabeth I. Also described is the varying types of land ownership — leasehold or freehold — by which the land was occupied. Two shields — one with a harp and the other with the cross of St George — are surrounded by the motto *Honi soit qui mal y pens*. The scale is about two miles to one inch and it was probably drawn by Francis Jobson. Jobson was one of the few cartographers who was physically present in Ireland and his work, along with that of Robert Lythe, was to be copied by, among others, John Speed in the preparation of his maps.

40

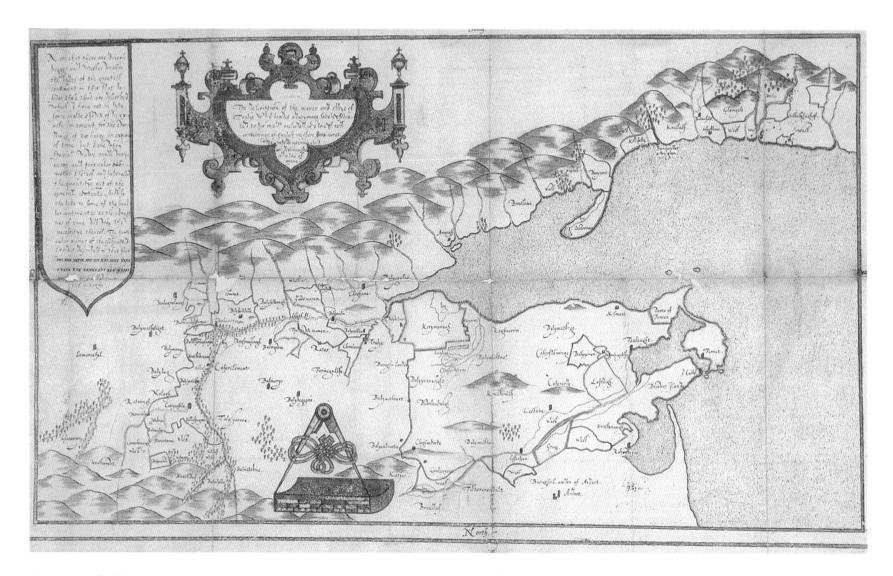

## Mayo 1587

**Left:** Covering the counties of Mayo and Sligo in northwest Connacht, this map records the advance and later the retreat of the Scottish mercenaries to and from Ardnaree in August and September 1586. The battle at Ardnaree was one of a number fought at this time as the Elizabethan administration sought to extend its influence into the areas still largely controlled by the native lords. Place names, baronies and woodlands are all delineated, and the map again shows evidence of annotation by Cecil. The cartouche gives fuller information regarding the events being portrayed.

## Tralee 1587

**Above:** Showing the manor and abbey of Tralee, the map also indicates the crown lands to the north (bottom) and south (top) of Tralee Bay. The scale is one mile to one inch. Now the county town of Kerry, Tralee had a strategic importance in that it guarded access to and from the Dingle peninsula. Its strategic importance is emphasized by the fact that, on two occasions (in 1643 and 1691), its defenders destroyed the town by fire rather than allow it to fall to the besieging forces. The result of this is that, today, there are no buildings in the town which predate the start of the 18th century.

## Blackwater Fort 1587

**Right, Above and Below:** This excellent contemporary illustration of one of the 16th century military installations portrays the castle at Blackwater in Armagh, County Tyrone, in Ulster. The map is dated March 27, 1587. Part of the plan is in perspective and part shows the groundplan; outside the castle are houses. Armagh occupies a strategic position just to the south of Lough Neagh and is situated at a major road intersection. It is the home today of both Roman Catholic Cardinal, head of the church in all Ireland, as well as the Protestant Archbishop. The name is derived from a legendary queen, Maccha, who, in the 3rd century AD, constructed a fort at Navan, about two miles to the east. The town's religious significance comes from the fact that St Patrick, Ireland's patron saint, founded a monastery here in the mid-5th century AD. This was the period when the English were seeking to expand their control over Ulster and, therefore, the holding of strategic locations was of vital importance in the exercise of this power.

## Sligo 1589

**Far Right:** Possibly drawn by John Browne, this map illustrates the coast of Sligo. It is endorsed by Sir Richard Bingham, the then president of Connacht, and dated April 20, 1589. Sligo is one of the five counties of the Province of Connacht. At the center of the map is the town of Sligo, the origins of which date back to the 6th century AD, and numerous other towns and abbeys are named. Of great significance in terms of the history of the period is the legend, north of the Barony of Carbery, which describes the presence of wrecked Spanish ships. It was in 1588 that King Philip II of Spain, who had been married to England's Queen Mary (Elizabeth's half-sister), decided to launch an invasion of Britain. The Armada was the result. Through a combination of stunning English seamanship and poor weather, the Spanish invasion came to nothing and the remaining ships were forced to sail round the British Isles before heading back towards Spain. In the course of this voyage numerous ships were destroyed by running aground or foundered in the heavy seas, and this legend records the fate of part of Philip's grand invasion fleet. At this time Sir Richard Bingham was seeking to expand English dominance to north Connacht and south Ulster, and this map is contemporaneous with his campaign.

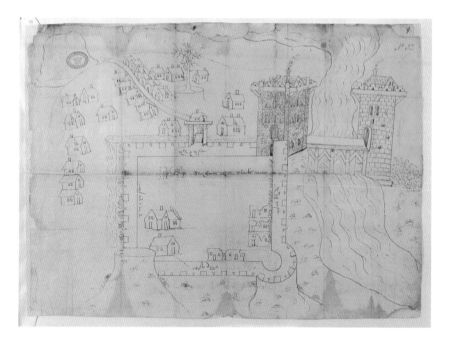

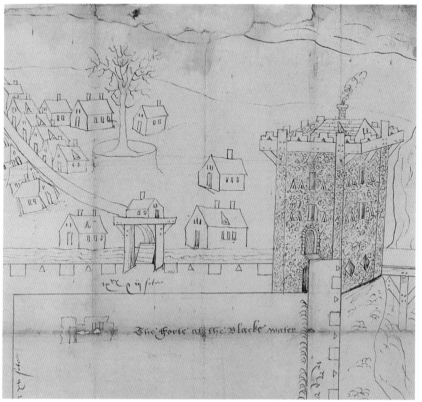

An antique hand-drawn map of County Tyrone and surrounding areas in Ireland.

Cormacke mc Baron
Broager to y' Erle
of Tyro

Con mc Erle
a baff

**Tyrone**

*(Her Majesty's State Paper Office stamp with crown)*

Fermanagh

mc guyre

Teghobogho

Collaghmore

Ni Ferma

the Flood

The Baromye
of Monohan

The Baromye
of Troughe

Cornehowe

pabryde  pt arte y
Hooke

Mc Mahon
Shee

Monahan abbey

Borye mc callos formos

Doggenan : 14 mile
fom mjlnachan :

Henry mc Mana
half fomley

Tyro

The Baromye
of Darleye

Clomes Abbey razed :
by Brien mc hugh oge :

Tyrehgan

Onaghe woods

Crossdalye where the
gallowglaffs inhabyte

Dromocagho

Brema

the hode

Brien mc hugh oge

The emetuffe

Kose bane chief :
The Baromye of
Ceymoxne

Patrib duff & & beholders yncloudid

Macheremolooghe

Machexymona

Towho
Noknown

fuse

Herny      Toighere

Donamayno :
cattoll :

The Baromye of
Damomoyne

Beeonye

The       Flood
kben mc       callys hous

Collobo mc brien
Somes

Clon cokawee

## Monaghan 1590

**Left:** Probably by John Browne and Jean Baptiste and endorsed with the date December 1590, this shows County Monaghan. Monaghan was one of the original nine counties of Ulster and is one of three (the other two being Donegal and Cavan) that became part of the Irish Free State at partition in 1922. The map shows the baronies and place names, with abbeys and other buildings illustrated by pictograms. As with a number of these 16th century maps, there have been additions and annotations to the map made by Sir William Cecil (by this date Lord Burghley).

## Cavan 1591

**Below:** One of the original nine counties of Ulster, and one of the three to be south of the border when Ireland was partitioned, Cavan is completely land-locked. The town of Cavan itself is portrayed, along with its castle, along with Lough Hearne (or the River Erne as it is known today). Although a scale is shown, the map's accuracy is sketchy, but it does highlight a number of structures in the vicinity including the Abbey of Golant. The name "Cavan" is derived from the Gaelic *An Cabhan*, meaning "Hollow Place." The town originally developed around an abbey, founded in 1300 and later destroyed. The entire town was destroyed by British forces in 1690 during the war between the supporters of the deposed King James II and those backing William of Orange. This map is also annotated by Sir William Cecil; it is his writing which comments "a plott of Cloneyss an abbey in McMahond's countrey." The map is possibly by John Browne and Jean Baptiste.

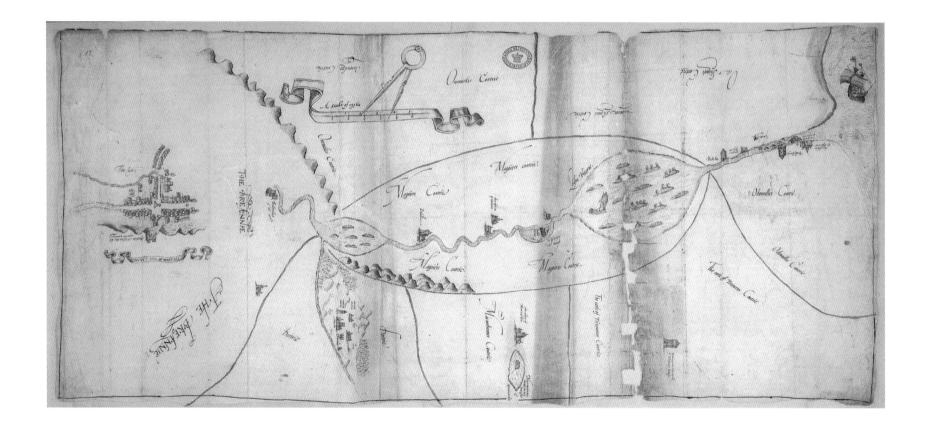

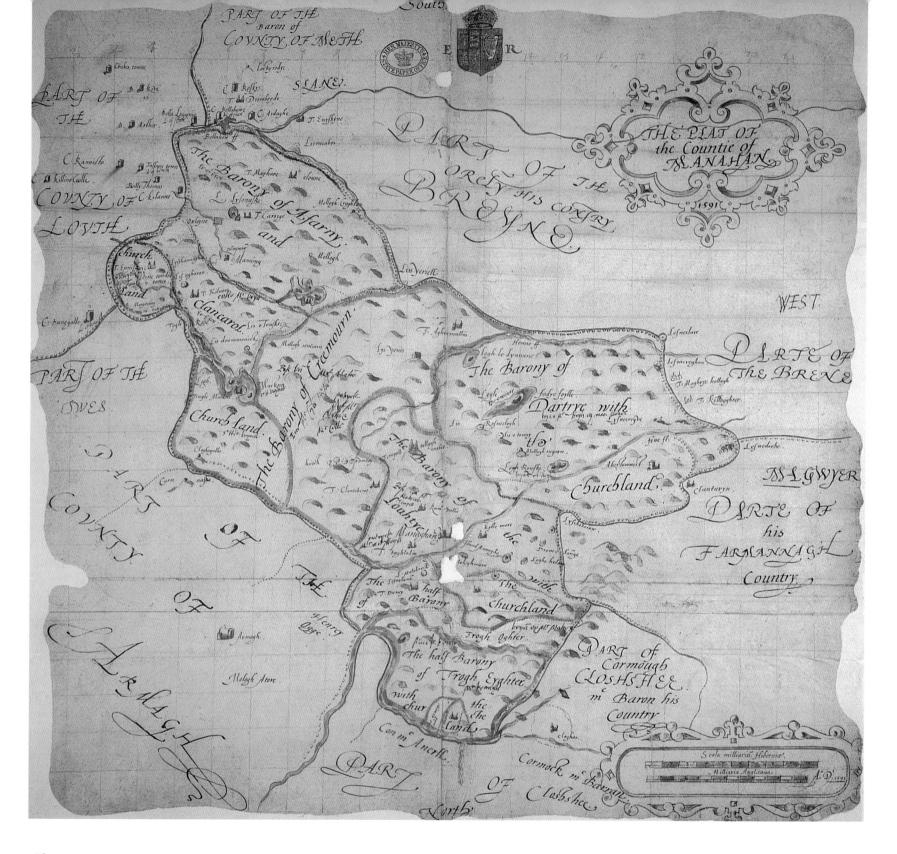

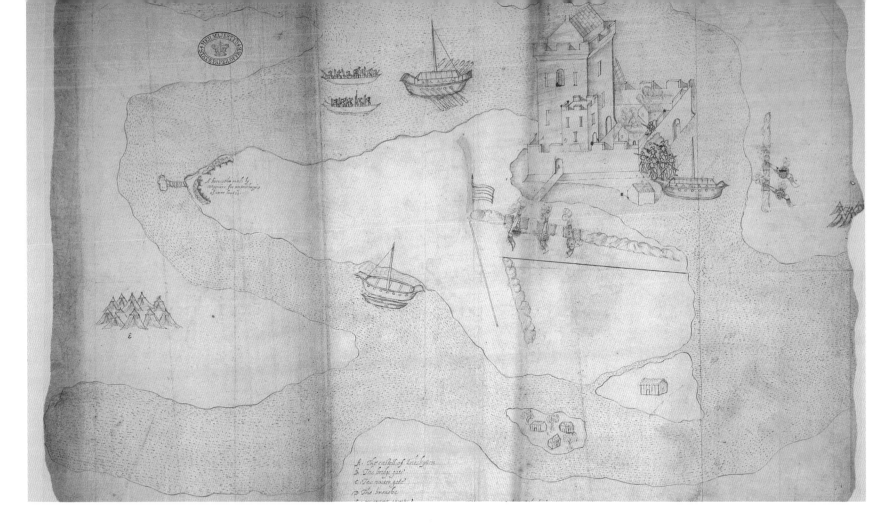

## Monaghan 1591

**Left:** The royal court of arms of Queen Elizabeth I — with the Irish harp alongside the lions of England surmounted by the crown — and the date, 1591, confirm that this map dates from the end of the 16th century. Possibly drawn by John Browne and Jean Baptiste to a scale of about three miles to one inch, it portrays County Monaghan. The axis of the map sees north at the bottom of the map and south at the top. Clearly identifiable are the various adjacent counties, such as Louth, and the division of the county itself into individual baronies. County Monaghan was one of the first parts of Ulster to see the Plantation established, during the 1550s, when land was seized from the Desmond family following an unsuccessful revolt. Note the amount of land allocated to the church; unlike England and Wales, where Elizabeth's father Henry VIII had been instrumental in the dissolution of the monasteries and the seizure by the crown of church lands, most of the religious houses in Ireland, outside the Pale (where Henry had wrought destruction), were dissolved after 1558 as royal power was extended.

## Enniskillen 1594

**Above:** This is a perspective view of the castle at Enniskillen, in County Fermanagh, showing Captain Bingham's camp, boats on the river, cannon firing at the castle and the English assault through a breach in the walls. It has been cited as an unfinished pen and ink copy of a map covering the siege of Enniskillen endorsed in September 1594. Enniskillen was an important strategic location on Lough Erne controlling the crossing between Ulster and Leitrim. Sir Richard Bingham, President of Connacht, was a powerful figure at the time in seeking to extend the power of the central government into north Connacht and Ulster during the period after 1589. The map was drawn contemporaneously with this action and portrays the English army endeavoring to capture a strategic strong-point. Enniskillen was to prove important in the late 17th century, when its Protestant majority refused to surrender to the deposed King James II and held out to provide William of Orange with one of the bridgeheads for his campaign against James II in Ireland between 1689 and 1691.

## Banagher c.1600

**Right:** Although undated, this map can be ascribed to the reign of Queen Elizabeth I. It portrays the town of Banagher and surrounding country in the area then known as King's County and which is now known as County Offaly, one of the constituent counties of the Province of Leinster. Banagher is situated alongside the River Shannon, to the south of Athlone. Drawn to a scale of 20 perches to one inch, the map shows houses in rough perspective as well as a church with yard. This settlement was located in the west of the county; in the east could be found the early Plantations of Offaly and Laois, which were first established in 1556. These Plantations were designed to seize land from the rebellious O'More and O'Connor families and transfer it to loyalist soldiers as a means of strengthening the border areas between the Pale proper and the native Irish.

## Carrickfergus c.1600

**Below Right:** Carrickfergus is situated on the north side of Belfast Lough, about seven miles northeast of Belfast. Prior to the emergence of Belfast as a major center in the 19th century, Carrickfergus was an important harbor in its own right. However, the dominant feature of the location — well illustrated in this perspective view of the location — was the castle. Known in mediaeval times as Kragfargys Castle, it was begun by John de Courcy, one of the Norman invaders, between 1180 and 1204. The location for the castle, built on a spur of black basalt that stretches into Belfast Lough and which was at the time almost an island, meant that it controlled Belfast Lough and was, therefore, an important strategic center. It was captured by King John in 1210 after a siege that lasted a year and was later, in 1316, to be captured by Scottish invaders. At the time that this map was produced, Carrickfergus had seen its defenses enhanced; however, it was allowed to decay after 1600 and was later to become a prison.

## Ulster 1602–03

**Far Right:** This and the following two maps show the Province of Ulster shortly before the death of Queen Elizabeth I and the accession of King James VI of Scotland to the English throne (as King James I). James VI was the son of Mary Queen of Scots — Elizabeth's cousin who had been executed while a prisoner in England for plotting against the English Queen — and with his accession the "United Kingdom" was born. It was not, however, until the start of the 18th century and the Act of Union that the Scottish parliament voted itself out of existence. The map is described as a "Generalle (sic) Description of Ulster." The cartouche includes the coat of arms of Charles Blount, Lord Mountjoy, who was the Lord Deputy of Ireland at the time. The scale is seven miles to an inch. The map also shows mountains and woods in perspective, as well as churches, houses or forts in elevation or plan. Also identified are the names of clans or chieftains; notable amongst these is the name O'Neill — one of the most influential of all the native Irish families.

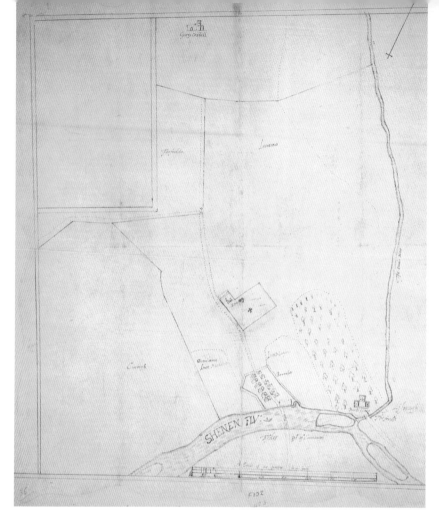

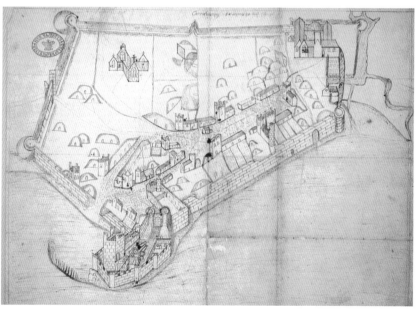

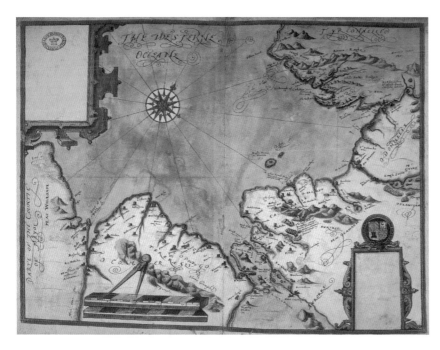

## Ulster 1602–3

**Far Left:** This map shows the southern part of the Province of Ulster; it is again part of a larger map. In the top right of the map appear the Royal Arms. These are significantly different to those of the modern Royal Family as they show the Fleur de Lys of France. At this time — and indeed for some years afterwards — the English crown lay claim to the throne of France; indeed at the time of this map's drafting, it was less than 50 years since England had lost its last permanent settlement on mainland Europe when the French recaptured Calais. Beneath the Royal Arms can be seen the arms of the Mountjoy family; Charles Blount, Baron Mountjoy was appointed governor in 1600 and he was at the forefront of the renewed English efforts to impose control. This section of the maps shows the area to the south of Lough Neagh, featuring places such as Dungannon. Note the emphasis upon fortifications; this map was drafted at the height of the Ulster Rebellion, shortly after the major defeat (in 1598) of the English forces at the Battle of the Yellow Ford and the English victory at Kinsale in 1601. It was after this victory — and the union of the English and Scottish crowns in 1603 with James VI of Scotland inheriting the English crown on the death of Elizabeth — that the massive colonization of the six counties, which were later to form Northern Ireland, commenced. This policy, adopted in 1608, was to have a major impact on the future of Ireland — an impact which continues to this day.

## Ulster 1602–3

**Above Left and Left (detail):** This is a detailed map of a section of the north-west part of the Province of Ulster. As with the earlier two previous maps, the arms of Lord Mountjoy are included; the blue belt surrounding the arms, with the Latin motto *Honi soit qui mal y pense*, symbolize Mountjoy's membership of the Order of the Garter — England's highest order of chivalry. The map, oriented with north to the top, shows the various counties which occupy the western approaches to Donegal Bay. Clearly identifiable are references to Mayo ("Parte of the Countie of Mayoe") and Sligo ("Terra [land] Sligo"). Again physical features are identified as are the names of clans or chieftains. The scale of the map is four miles to one inch.

THE BARONIE OF
CLINAWLEY.

HER MAJESTYES
STAPLE PAPER OFFICE

Leytrim

Leytrim

Leytrim

Leytrim

Lough Erne

Knocknyny

Cullmtragh

Oysay

holeroan

Coagban

mullyyar

aghcornalt

goseloddey

killuonge

Neue

aghrm

killertiue

gorteranna

kmullalostie

Lough

Carronoueleu

Carrowdrmale

Carrongarrach

guoyluellen

Carronmucklau

Crottan

moycharne

aghboe

gortiquon

molladone

Maghery Boy

aroroncragh

tullacha

ballenebegush

quoylarahid

lisdonorich

dorvagskie

dromberrih

tullagonxin

mollanebanga

legneycng

montagh

aghleagh

amesmore

tullagho

Craghagron

liscollorry

Shankill

shankill

drishm

rasdorny

Seseagh

glecagh

dromsrollos

doonboy

gortdonnoegho

niellamerker

raballan

moyleile

moylehles

Landes of Elemish

reyne

mullalougs

Landes of Lisgoole

trelicke

re

MAGHERY

Boy

Landes of Tobundis

Imskillin

MAGHERY-
STEFFANA

52

## Clanawley c.1609

**Left:** This is a map of the Barony of "Clinawley" (Clanawley), which was one of the baronies established in County Fermanagh in 1609 as part of the process of creating the Ulster Plantation. Tenancies for Servitors and native Irish were permitted in certain circumstances in these baronies. To the north lay the barony of Magheraby, to the southeast the barony of Knockninny and to the east the barony of Maghera-Stephana. The map includes the names of properties and information regarding bogs and woodland. Perspective views of churches, forts, hills and mountains are also included. This map and those that follow dated 1609 were produced by the Commission established on July 19, 1608 to survey the counties of Ulster; following their report, the land was granted to the British "Undertakers" in April and May 1610.

## Clankee c.1609

**Above:** County Cavan was one of the original nine counties of the Province of Ulster and is today one of three that are situated in the Republic of Ireland. Clankee ("Clanchy") was one of number of baronies established in Cavan and was the easternmost of them, forming a border with the neighboring counties of Louth and Monaghan. Clankee was one the Jacobean Plantation areas established from 1609 with Scottish "Undertakers;" again, parcels of land, ranging in extent from 1,000 to 2,000 acres, were created for tenants arriving from either England or Scotland.

## Clankelly c.1609

**Right (detail) and Below:** This is a map of "The Baronie of Clancally" in County Fermanagh, one of seven baronies created in Fermanagh and located at the extreme east of the county, bordering Monaghan. Clankelly was one of two baronies in Fermanagh — the other being Lurg — which saw the Plantation established in 1609 by English "Undertakers" exclusively for tenants from England or Scotland. The area described as "Marghery Staffana" is a further barony in Fermanagh — Maghera-Stephana — while between Clankelly itself and Lough Erne to the south was the northern part of a third barony, that of Knockninny. Monaghan to the east had been "Planted" following the Earl of Desmond's revolt in the previous century.

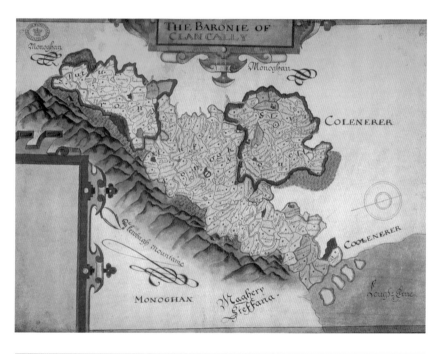

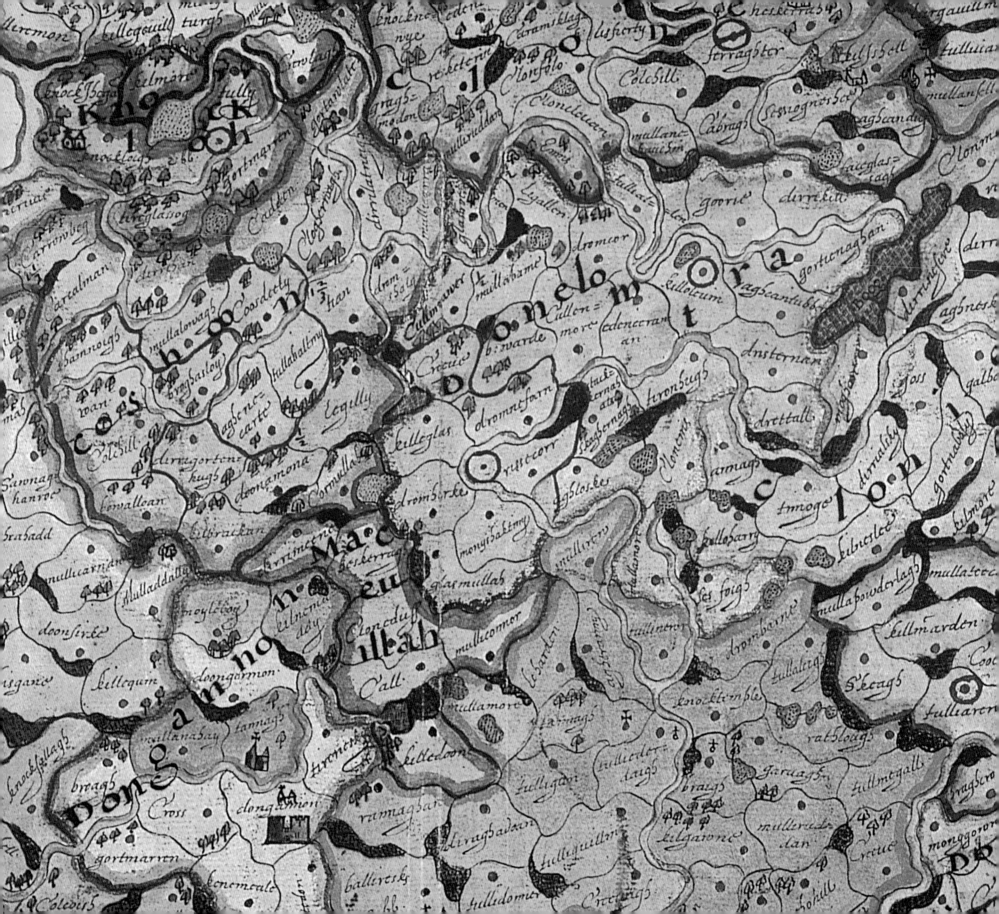

# Dungannon c.1609

**Left (detail), Below (detail), Above Right and Right:** Dungannon, in County Tyrone, is located just to the west of Lough Neagh. These two maps, which are contemporary with the creation of the Ulster Plantation in the early years of the 17th century, show adjacent parts of the Barony of Dungannon. Although the two maps are complementary, it is clear that they were produced by two different cartographers. Not only is the script of the main legend different but, more significantly, the actual presentation of the information is also at variance. In one aspect both maps are, however, consistent and that is the fact that they are both allied with south towards the top of the map and north towards the bottom; Lough Neagh is actually to the east of Dungannon and Armagh to the south. Dungannon was one of the Plantations created where the land could be held in certain circumstances by Servitors or Native Irish. Servitors were Englishmen who had fulfilled a service to the Crown, either through military or civil duty. Once Servitors had acquired rights to the land they were expected to ensure that any native tenants behaved themselves while also encouraging migration from Britain. The native Irish occupiers were those who had proved themselves loyal to the crown; land was, therefore, seen as a reward for support of English authority.

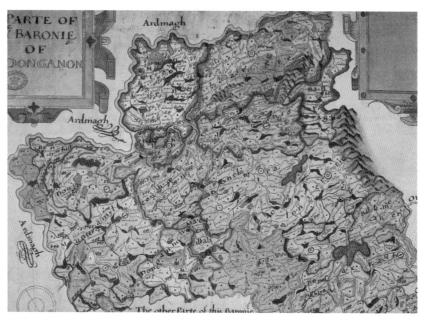

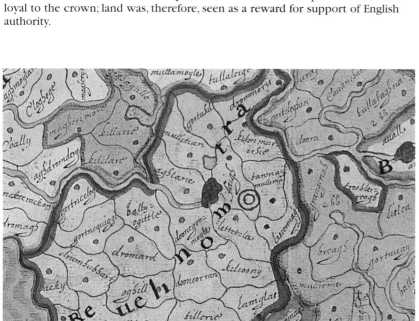

## Knockninny c.1609

**Right and Far Right (detail):** The barony of Knockninny, in County Fermanagh, was in two parts, to the west and east of Upper Lough Erne. This first of two maps recording the creation of the barony in 1609 portrays that part of the barony to the east of the Lough. The map is aligned, approximately, with north towards the top and with Upper Lough Erne forming the southwest border of the barony. To the northeast is the barony of "Clancallie" (Clankelly) and to the north "Magherie Staffana" (Maghera Staphana). To the east lies Monaghan and to the south, Cavan. The Plantation in Knockninny was undertaken by Scots with tenants coming from either England or Scotland. The map includes information on place names as well as physical features — churches and so on — in perspective.

## Knockninny c.1609

**Below and Below Right (detail):** This is the second half of the barony of Knockninny, located on the west side of Upper Lough Erne. Its alignment is approximately with east towards the bottom and west towards the top. To the south lies the barony of Loughtee and to the west that of Tullyhaw (both in Cavan), and to the north, Clanawley (also in County Fermanagh).

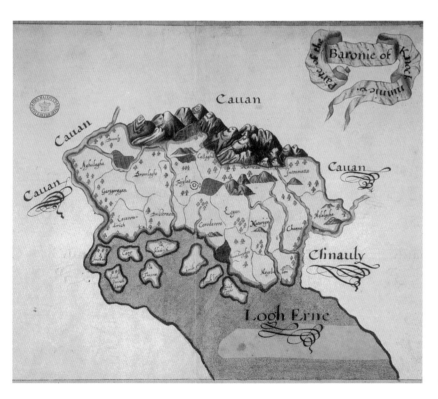

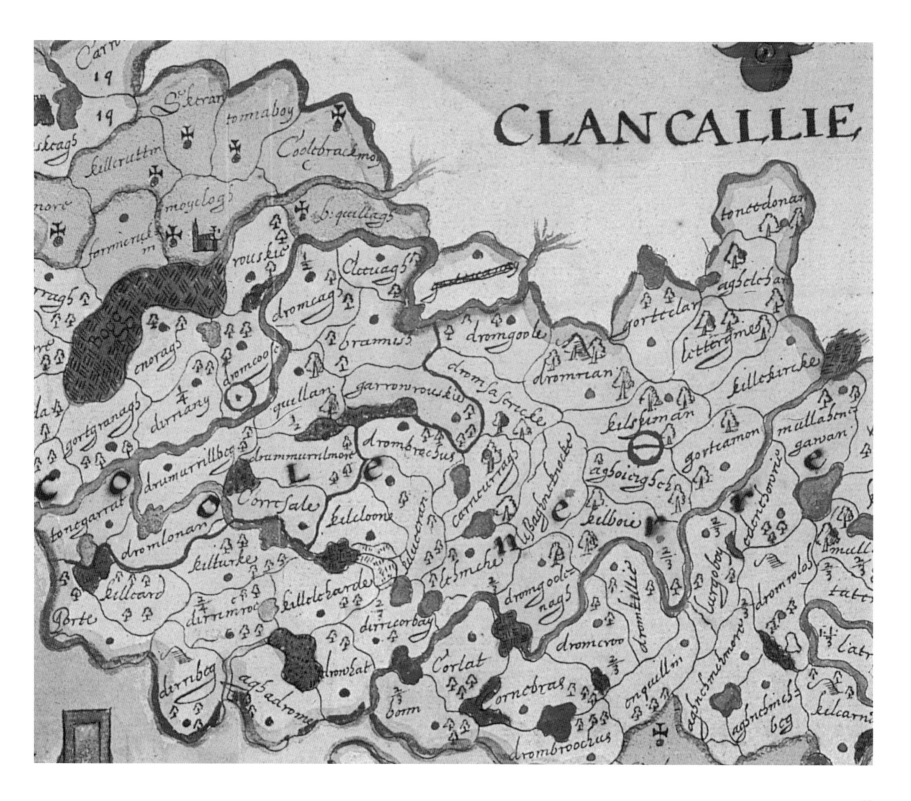

CLANCALLIE,

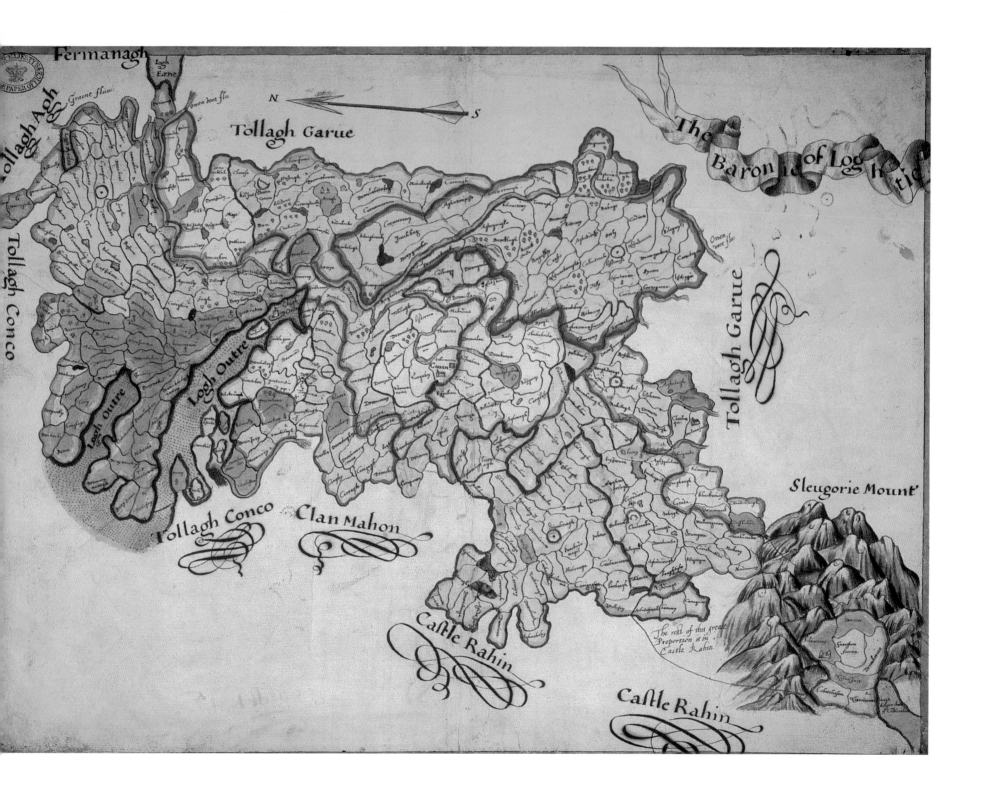

Fermanagh

Logh Erne

Graine flan:

Tollagh Agh

Tollagh Garue

The Baronie of Loghtie

Tollagh Conco

Logh Outre

Tollagh Garue

Tollagh Conco    Clan Mahon

Sleugorie Mount

Castle Rahin

The rest of this great Proportion is in Castle Rahin.

Castle Rahin

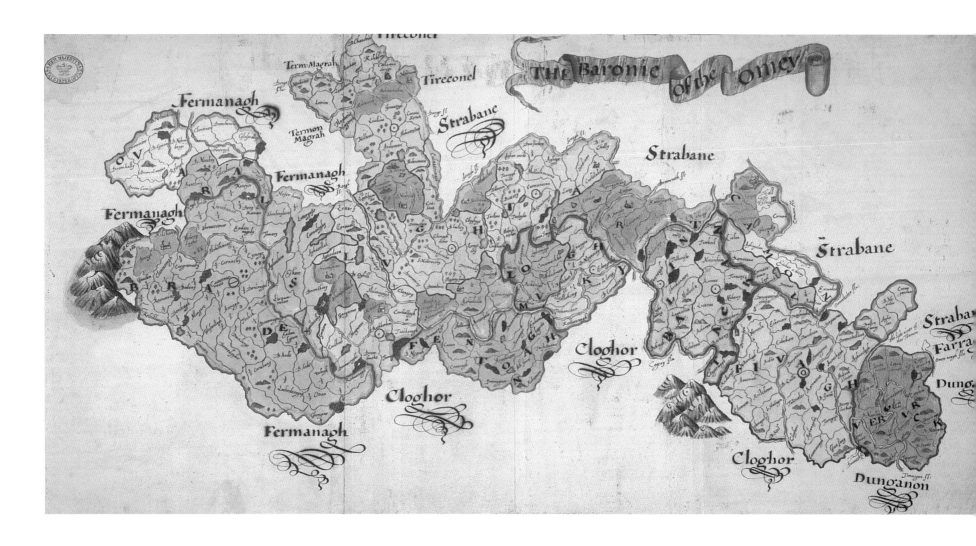

## Loughtee c.1609

**Left:** This is a second barony created within Cavan; "Loughtie" (Logthee) was sited with Lough Oughter to the north and Lough Gowna, linked by the River Erne, to the south. Among settlements in the barony was the town of Cavan itself. As with the Barony of Clankee, the Barony of Loughtee was established for Scottish "Undertakers" as part of the Ulster Plantation from 1609. The tenants were planned to be settlers from either England or Scotland.

## Omagh c.1609

**Above:** "Omey" (Omagh) was one of the baronies created in County Tyrone; the Plantation was undertaken by English owners with settlers coming from Scotland and England. It was surrounded on the north by the barony of Strabane, on the east by Mountjoy and Dungannon, on the south by Clogher and by County Fermanagh and on the west by County Donegal.

## Oneilland c.1609

**Right and Below (detail):** Described as "Parte of the Barony of Oneilan" this map illustrates part of County Armagh. Note the churches portrayed in perspective (see detail below). Armagh is one of the six counties of Ulster which today form the modern Northern Ireland. Oneilland is that part of the county which is located to the south of Lough Neagh. This map is contemporaneous with the start of the colonization of this part of Ulster in 1609, which saw English "Undertakers" creating estates of between 1,000 and 2,000 acres for English or Scottish tenants. The creation of these estates became known as the "Ulster Plantation."

## Strabane 1609

**Far Right:** This map of the "Baronie of Strabane" illustrates that part of County Tyrone situated alongside the River Foyle to the south of Londonderry. Tyrone is one of the six counties of Ulster which now form Northern Ireland; the border between the Republic of Ireland and Northern Ireland now runs along the Rover Foyle at this point with County Donegal, another of the original nine counties of Ulster, situated to the west in the Republic.

## Tullyhaw c.1609

**Right:** This a third map portraying a barony created in County Cavan at the start of the 17th century for Scottish "Undertakers." "Tollagh Aghe" (Tullyhaw) was the westernmost of the Cavan baronies and was located adjacent to County Leitrim. It is interesting to note that the county boundaries were still not settled as one parcel of land; it is noted that "This lande is in controversie betweene this countie and the county of Leytrim." The map shows various physical features, including bogs and woodland, while churches and mountains are shown in perspective.

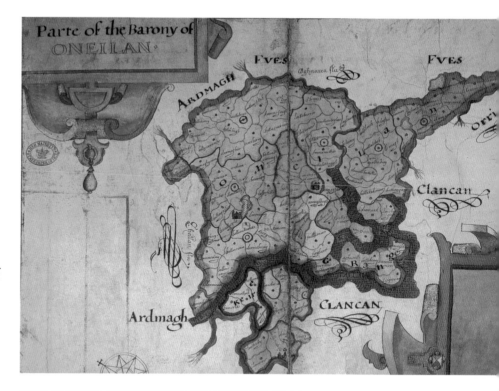

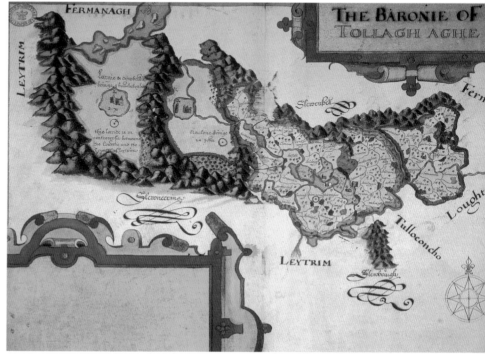

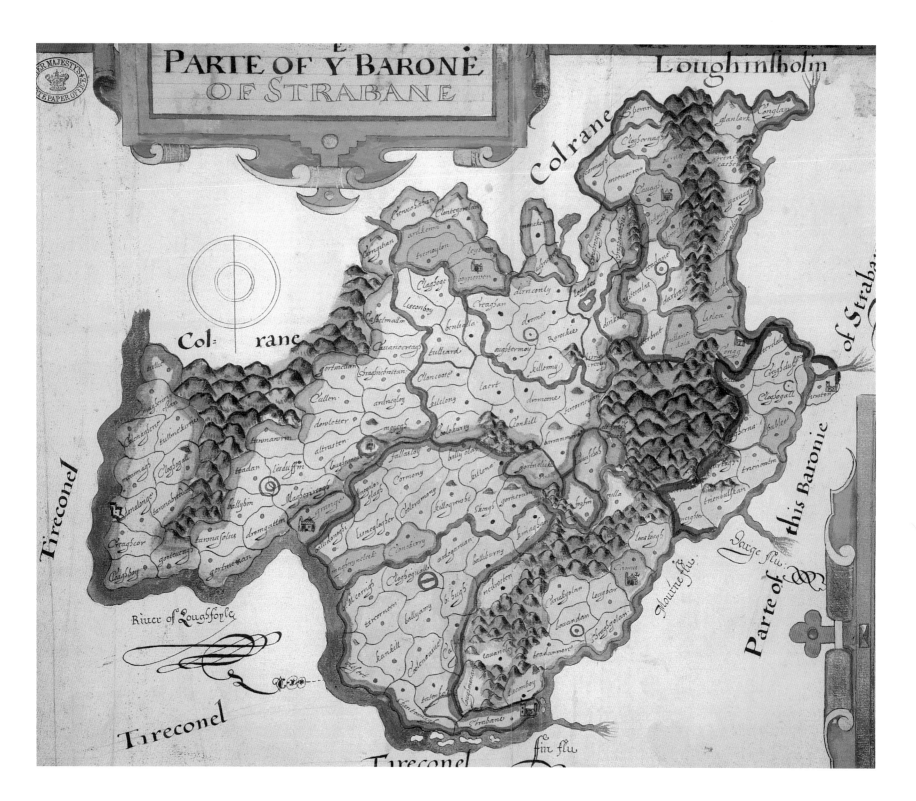

# PARTE OF Y BARONE
## OF STRABANE

Loughinsholin

Colrane

Col-rane

Tireconel

of Strabane

Parte of this Baronie

Riuer of Loughfoyle

Tireconel

Tireconel

fin flu

## Ireland c.1610

**Left:** Drawn to a scale of nine miles to one inch, this map shows the whole island of Ireland, oriented with north towards the right, at the end of the first decade of the 17th century. While the map is clearly identifiable — including information on towns, castles, nobles and landowners — the compiler, John Norden, has elongated the north/south scale, thus distorting the actual shape of the island. Typical of much of the contemporary map work, Norden based his version of the map upon one drawn in 1599 by Boazio. It was part of a sequence of maps drawn by Norden and dedicated to the Earl of Salisbury. John Norden (1548–1626) was one of the pioneers of English cartography. From the start of the last decade of the 16th century he endeavored, unsuccessfully, to produce a series of guidebooks for the various counties; however, he lacked the financial backing to make a success of this and then concentrated on the drawing of larger maps. Baptista Boazio (1588–1606) was an Italian by birth who came to England; his much-copied map of Ireland is perhaps his most best-known work.

## Augher c.1610

**Right:** This and the next three illustrations are taken from a volume compiled by John Norden, one of the greatest of early 17th century English map makers. Called *A Description of Ireland,* it was produced in the early 17th century and dedicated to the Earl of Salisbury. This first illustration shows the castle of Augher ("Agher") in County Tyrone. Tyrone was one of the nine original counties of the Province of Ulster and is one of the sixth that now form Northern Ireland; it is situated to the west of Lough Neagh and is sandwiched between Fermanagh and Derry. Augher is situated just to the north of the boundary between Tyrone and Monaghan to the west of Dungannon.

## Charlemont c.1610

**Center Right, Above:** Charlemont ("Charlemount") is situated in Armagh on the border with County Tyrone; the Blackwater forms the boundary between the two. River crossings were important strategic locations and the proximity of the bridge at this point with the castle is clearly evident here.

## Mulline c.1610

**Far Right:** Of the three forts illustrated here, Moungeye ("Mountjoy") and Mulline are both in County Tyrone; the third cannot be readily identified. Mountjoy Fort, situated on the west side of Lough Neagh to the northeast of Dungannon, was one of the forts constructed by Lord Mountjoy following his suppression of O'Neill's rising. It is interesting to note that the Lough, called "Eaugh" here, is also described as "Lough Sidnye;" Sir Henry Sidney (1529–1586) was governor of Ireland from 1565 until 1571 and again from 1575 until 1578. Initially, during his time in control, he adopted a military solution to Ulster and in Munster and encourages colonization; later he sought a more conciliatory approach and, temporarily, caused colonization to cease. The fort at Mulline is also described as the "New Fort" on the Blackwater, which flows into Lough Neagh from the southwest, passing through Monaghan and Armagh *en route*. Lough Neagh, with an area of 150 square miles, is the largest lake in the British Isles.

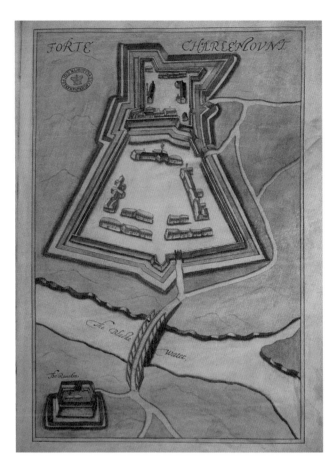

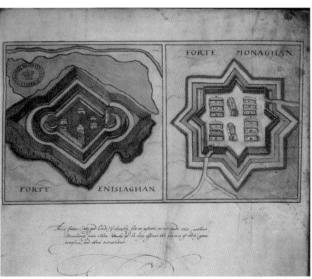

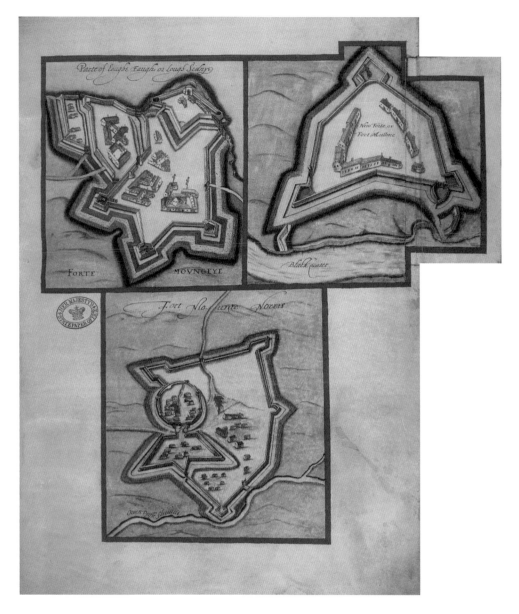

## Monaghan/Enislaghan c.1610

**Left:** This illustration portrays two forts: Enislaghan in Armagh and Monaghan in Monaghan. At the time that these maps were compiled, both formed part of Ulster; today, however, Armagh is in Northern Ireland and Monaghan in the Republic. It is interesting to note from the illustrations — an aspect only achievable as a result of the use of perspective to delineate the buildings rather than a simple plan — that the fort at Enislaghan appears to have been constructed with wooden stockades.

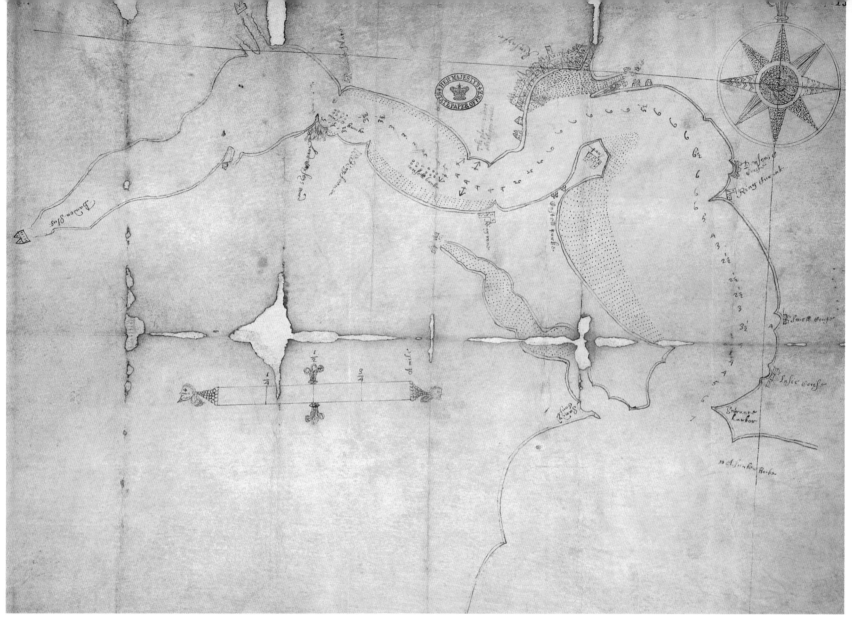

## *Kinsale 1637*

**Above:** This is a chart of the harbor and of the River Bandon at Kinsale with soundings of the channel to a point two miles above the town. The map, dated October 1637 (during the reign of King Charles I), was drawn to a scale of one-fifth of a mile to one inch. Kinsale is located on the south coast of Ireland to the west of Cork. In 1601, the area was invaded by the Spanish in support of the Irish in their campaign against the English. Following the Irish defeat, the Spaniards surrendered. The English victory at Kinsale is followed by the Flight of the Earls, when many of the native Irish leaders fled abroad, and confirmed that Ireland remained firmly under English rule. In the following year, 1602, Kinsale was declared an English town from which all native Irish were barred; it was not until the late 18th century that this restriction was lifted. Kinsale's importance was also reflected in the fact that it was a base for the Royal Navy.

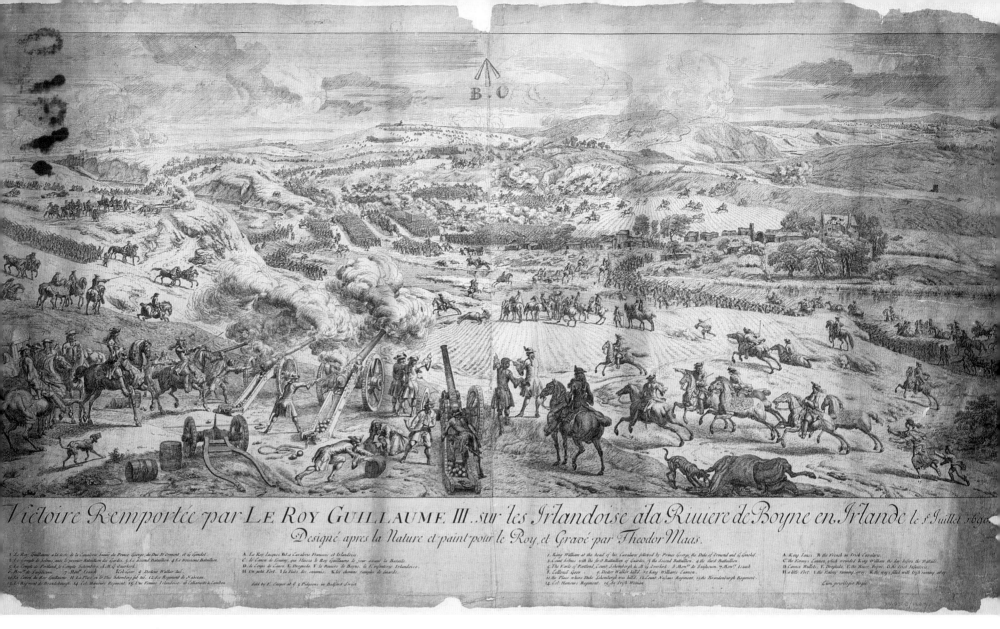

*Victoire Remportée par LE ROY GUILLAUME III sur les Irlandoise ala Riuiere de Boyne en Irlande le 1 Juillet 1690*

*Designé apres la Nature et paint pour le Roy, et Gravé par Theodor Maas.*

# Boyne 1690

**Above:** Of all the battles fought during the struggles in Ireland, none is more famous — or infamous — than the Battle of the Boyne, fought on July 1, 1690. This is a dramatic reconstruction of the battle engraved by Theodor Maas. Although the title is in French, the reference tables below are in both French and English. Following William of Orange's successful Glorious Revolution, which saw the Catholic king James II forced from the throne, James retreated to Ireland where he was certain to receive more sympathetic support and where he hoped to consolidate power before attempting to regain his throne. William responded to the threat by landing in Ireland and marching southwards. Located in County Meath, the crossing over the River Boyne was a strategic point which James II had to hold if the army of William was not to succeed in its advance on Dublin to the south. James's army was ranged along the south side of the river and,

theoretically, this should have enhanced his chances of defeating William. However, William sent part of his forces to cross the river further west, thereby outflanking the pro-Stuart army and inflicting a major defeat upon James. This was not the final defeat of the Jacobites in Ireland — the campaign continued into 1691, with sieges at Limerick and the Battle of Aughrim — but it did mark the fact that the balance of military power in Ireland had shifted irrevocably towards the supporters of William. It is the Battle of the Boyne that is marked by many of the Protestants in Northern Ireland during the marching season and, more than 300 years after the actual event, is still a cause of friction between the rival traditions.

# Kinsale 1691

**Right:** The strategic importance of Kinsale again became apparent at the end of the 17th century when in March 1689 the recently deposed King James II arrived at the town from France in order to try and re-establish his power. This map is contemporaneous with the campaign being fought in Ireland between the forces loyal to James II and those of the new monarch William III. The map was produced for the French — hence the legend *Plan de la ville et Forts de Kinsale* ("plan of the town and forts of Kinsale") — and was produced to a scale of 400 feet to one inch. The French king, Louis XIV, was an enthusiastic supporter of James II and provided assistance in James' efforts to regain the throne. Following the defeat of the pro-Stuart army at the Battle of the Boyne on July 1, 1690, the army of William of Orange marched southwards, besieging and capturing Cork in September 1690 and taking Kinsale after a short siege in the following month. By this date James II had again fled into exile, leaving his army to campaign without him until the final settlement with the Treaty of Limerick in October 1691.

# Dublin 1722

**Far Right:** Copied by John Bastide, this map shows the plan and elevation of the Horse and Foot Barracks at Dublin. The historic core of Dublin was the walled city on the south bank of the River Liffey with the castle at its southeast corner. By the end of the 17th century, the city had spread across to the north bank and during the 18th century continued to expand both north and south. As the capital of Ireland and the pivotal location for British power on the island, Dublin was well provided with public buildings as well as facilities to accommodate the military presence.

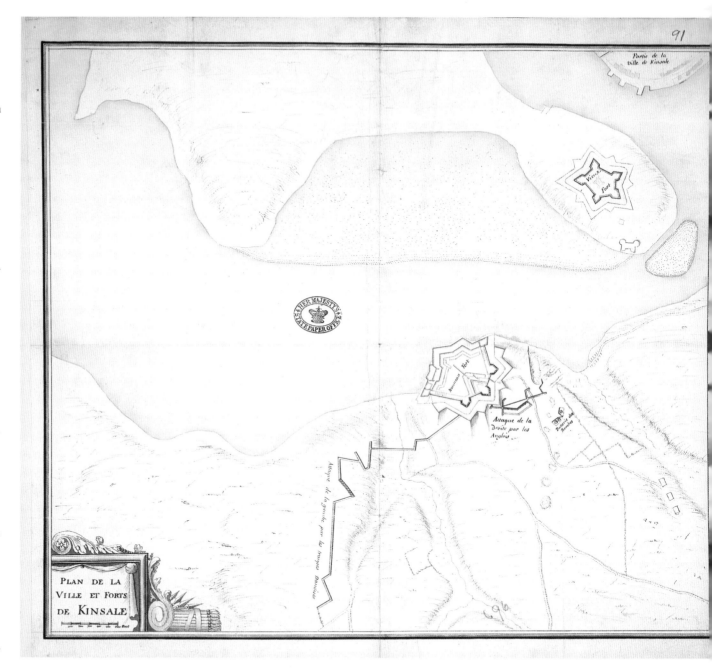

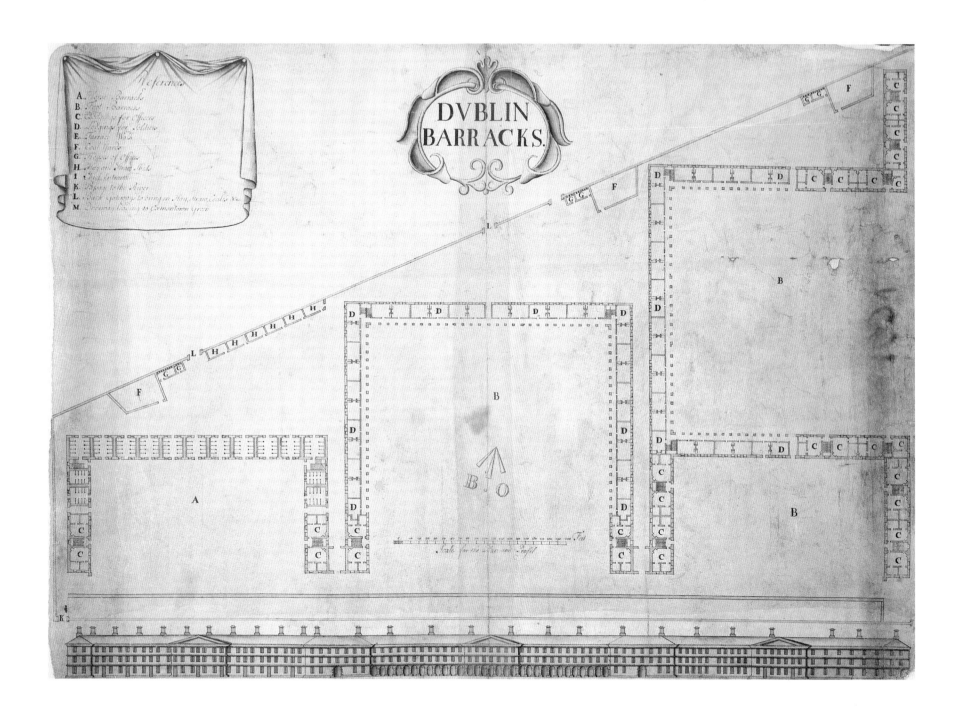

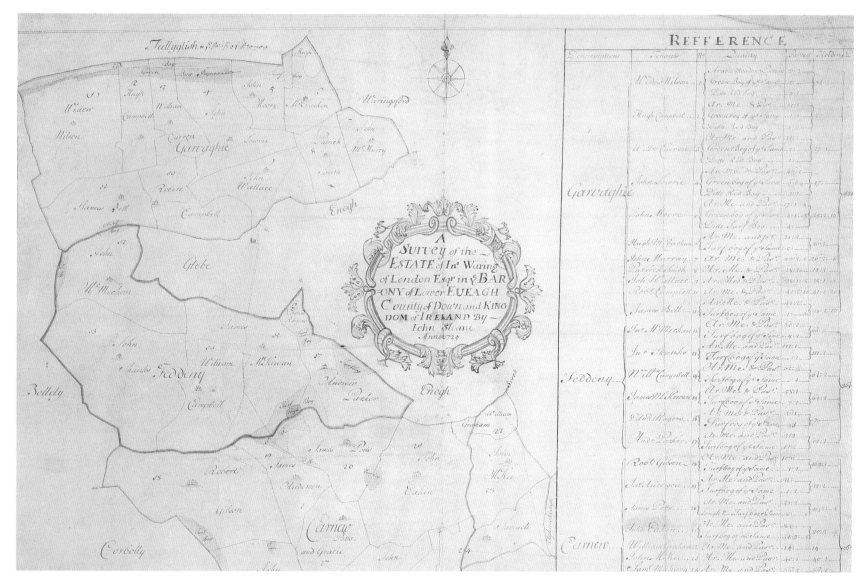

## Lower Iveagh 1725

**Above:** This is a survey of the estate of John Waring, Esq., of London in Garvaghy, Carnew and Fedany. Lower Iveagh is part of County Down. The scale of the map which was surveyed by John Sloane in 1725, is 40 Irish perches to one inch. The table gives a full list of the tenant farmers, the quality of the land and the acreages concerned.

## Ireland c.1759

**Right (detail):** Drawn to a scale of about 13 miles to one inch and published by Thomas Jefferys, this map was included in Lord Townshend's dispatch of October 15, 1770. It portrays the provinces, counties, baronies, cities, towns and principal villages. Also illustrated are the locations for cavalry and infantry barracks. George Townshend (1724–1807), was Viceroy in Ireland from October 14, 1767 until he was recalled on November 30, 1772. A prominent politician in Britain, he had a crucial role in Ireland in helping to reduce the power and patronage of the so-called "Undertakers" and in strengthening British control. Townshend succeeded as the fourth Viscount Townshend in 1764, and was created a Marquess in 1786.

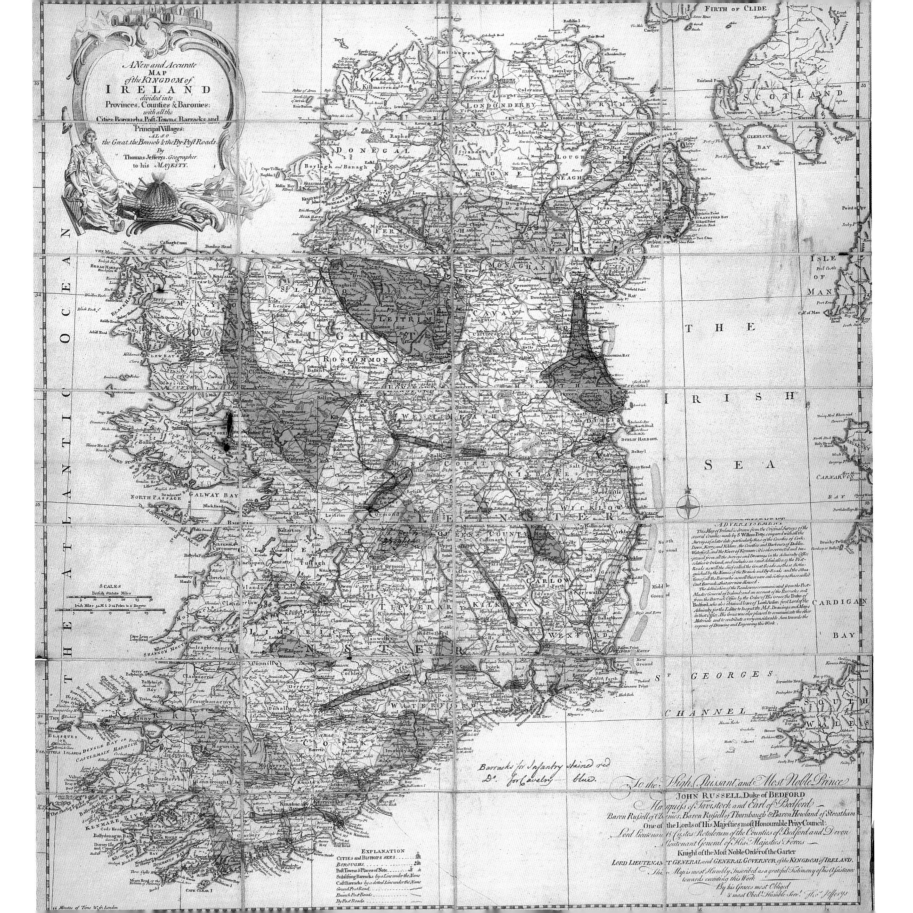

A New and Accurate MAP of the KINGDOM of IRELAND divided into Provinces, Counties & Baronies; with all the Cities, Boroughs, Post-Towns, Barracks, and Principal Villages: ALSO the Great, the Branch & the By-Post Roads By Thomas Jefferys, Geographer to his MAJESTY.

SCOTLAND

FIRTH OF CLIDE

ISLE OF MAN

THE IRISH SEA

ST. GEORGES. CHANNEL

CARDIGAN BAY

SOUTH WALES

THE ATLANTIC OCEAN

ULSTER

CONNAUGHT

LEINSTER

MUNSTER

DONEGAL
LONDONDERRY
ANTRIM
TYRONE
FERMANAGH
MONAGHAN
ARMAGH
DOWN
CAVAN
LEITRIM
SLIGO
MAYO
ROSCOMMON
GALWAY
LONGFORD
WESTMEATH
MEATH
DUBLIN
KILDARE
KINGS COUNTY
QUEENS COUNTY
WICKLOW
CARLOW
KILKENNY
WEXFORD
TIPPERARY
CLARE
LIMERICK
KERRY
CORK
WATERFORD

GALWAY BAY
CLEW BAY
DONEGAL BAY
DINGLE BAY
KENMARE RIVER

ADVERTISEMENT
This Map of Ireland is drawn from the Original Surveys of the several Counties made by S.r William Petty, compared with all the Surveys of a later date, particularly those of the Counties of Cork, Down, Kerry, and Kildare, the Counties and Harbours of Dublin, Waterford, and the River of Kinmare; it is also corrected and improved from all the Surveys and Drawings in the Admiralty Office relative to Ireland, and includes an exact delineation of the Post Roads, as well the chief called the Great Roads, as those distinguished by the Names of the Branch and By-Roads, and the Situations of all the Barracks as well those now subsisting as those called Cost Barracks, that are now disused.

EXPLANATION
CITIES and BISHOPS SEES
BOROUGHS
Post Towns & Places of Note
Subsisting Barracks by a Line under the Name
Cost Barracks by a dotted Line under the Name
Ground Post Road
Branch Post Road
By Post Roads

8 SCALES
British Statute Miles
Irish Miles

Barracks for Infantry stained red
D.o for Cavalry — blue.

To the High, Puissant, and Most Noble Prince
JOHN RUSSELL, Duke of BEDFORD
Marquiss of Tavistock and Earl of Bedford
Baron Russell of Cheneis, Baron Russell of Thornhaugh & Baron Howland of Streatham
One of the Lords of His Majesties most Honourable Privy Council:
Lord Lieutenant & Custos Rotulorum of the Counties of Bedford and Devon
Lieutenant General of His Majesties Forces
Knight of the Most Noble Order of the Garter
LORD LIEUTENANT GENERAL and GENERAL GOVERNOR of the KINGDOM of IRELAND.
This Map is most Humbly Inscribed as a grateful Testimony of his Assistance towards executing this Work
By his Graces most Obliged & most Obed.t Humble Serv.t Tho.s Jefferys

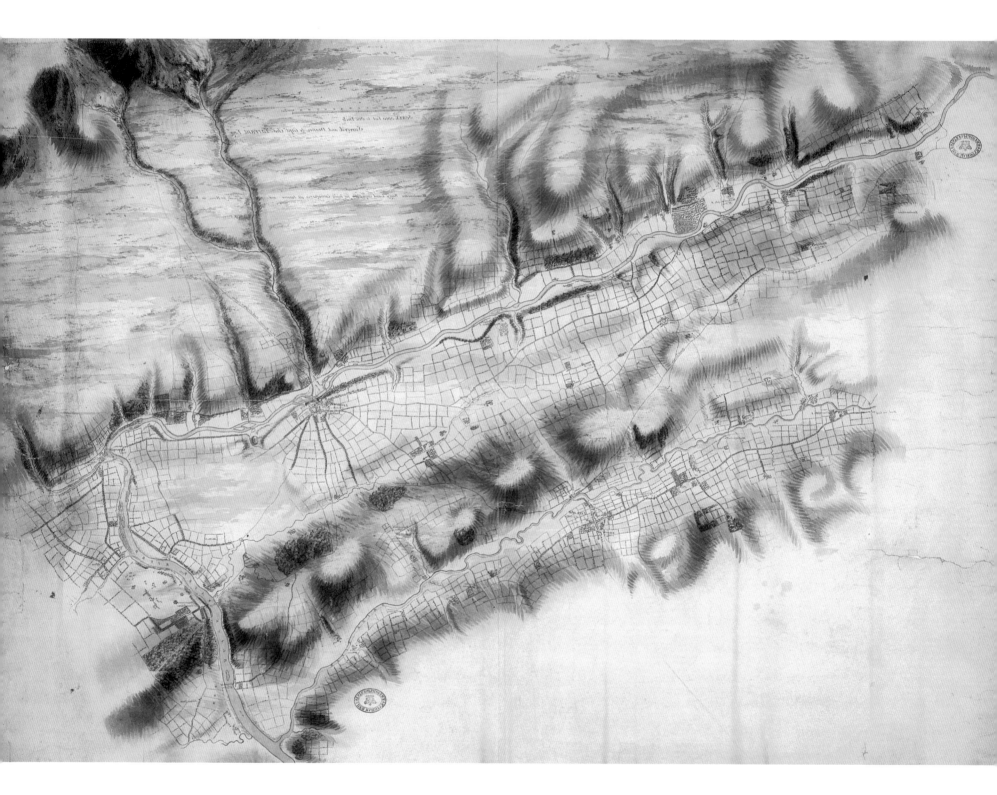

74

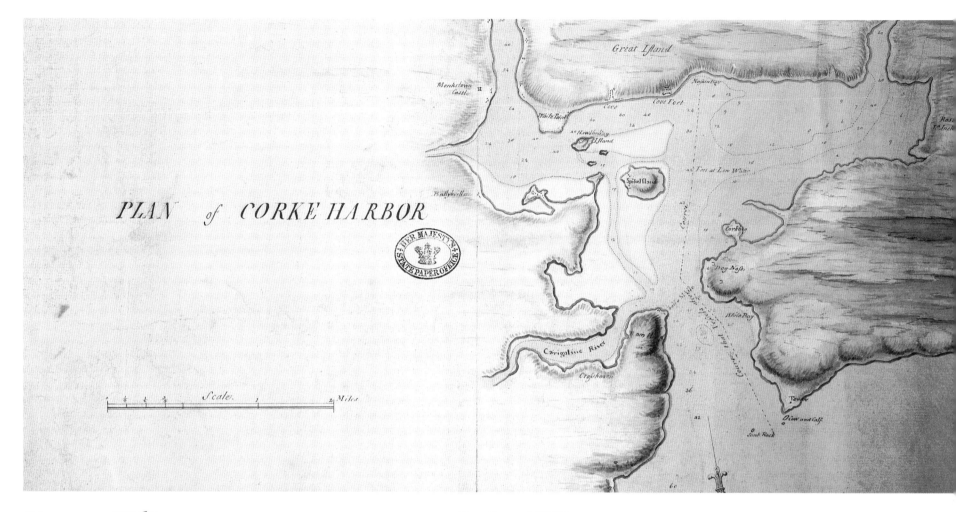

*PLAN of CORKE HARBOR*

Scale. Miles

## Lismore 1760

**Left:** Situated in the County of Waterford, in the Province of Munster, Lismore — *Lios Mor Muchuda* — lies on the Blackwater about halfway between Waterford and Cork. This is a detailed map of the rivers Blackwater and Bride as well as the country around Lismore. The scale is 3,000 feet to one inch. The map predates the construction of the bridge, built in 1775, which is still extant today. It was in the early 7th century that a monastery was first built at Lismore. Today, Lismore Castle probably occupies the site of the monastery. First constructed in the 12th century, it passed in the early years of the 17th century into the hands of Richard Boyle, who was later first Earl of Cork and whose son, Robert, was a scientist who produced Boyle's Law. Today, the castle — extended in the 19th century — belongs to the Duke of Devonshire, one of the leading aristocrats in Britain who also owns the famous Chatsworth House in Derbyshire. The influence of the Boyle family is also reflected in the 17th century St Carthage's Cathedral, which was built for Richard Boyle and incorporated part of an older church. The church, which is now a National Monument, was modified in the 19th century.

## Cork c.1770

**Above:** Cork was and remains one of the most important harbors in Ireland. Although the city appears to be inland, it is in fact built on an arm of the sea, which provides an excellent natural harbor. Access to the sea is via a strait called Passage West which passes round Spike Island and in between the defensive points of Camden and Carlisle forts. Through the town flows the River Lee and the original settlement, dating back to the 7th century, was on a small island in the middle of the river, with, appropriately, North Channel to the north and South Channel to the south. Scaled at about three-quarters of a mile to one inch, this map illustrates the harbor towards the end of the third quarter of the 18th century at the time when Lord Townshend was Viceroy.

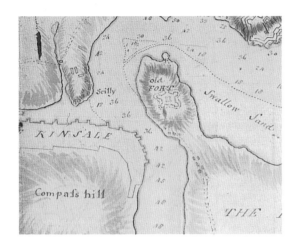

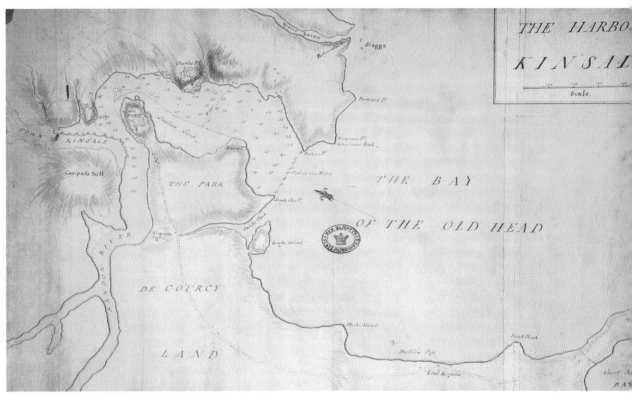

## Kinsale c.1770

**Above (details) and Above Right:** Contemporaneous with the preceding map and drawn to a scale of 1,200 feet to one inch, this illustration portrays the harbor, with soundings, at Kinsale, to the west of Cork. By this date, Kinsale was coming towards the period when it was prohibited for native Irish to reside in the town. Of those from the town, one of the most famous was William Penn who was to achieve prominence in the future United States of America as the founder of Pennsylvania.

## Cork 1781

**Right:** While the 18th century was an era of increasing prosperity in Ireland and was, relatively, one of stability in relationships between government and population, there were events elsewhere in the world which had an impact on Irish affairs. It was in 1776 that the Thirteen Colonies of Britain's North American Empire declared independence, leading to the War of Independence. This map was produced during that war. Although Britain and France did not undertake hostilities in Europe at this time, war was declared and the latter did provide considerable support to the rebels. It was the threat posed in Europe from France and Spain, both of which had suffered heavy defeats and consequent loss of territory in North America and the Caribbean earlier in the 18th century, which forced Britain to accede to the demands of the Thirteen Colonies for independence. Cork, as a major harbor, was a critical point for the British supply lines of both naval and civilian vessels and was, as a result, well defended. This map, drawn at the same time as the War of Independence in the Thirteen Colonies was drawing to a close, shows the range of guns defending the harbor. It was one of a series of maps prepared by Lieutenant-Colonel Charles Vallancey, Royal Engineers, whose report they accompanied.

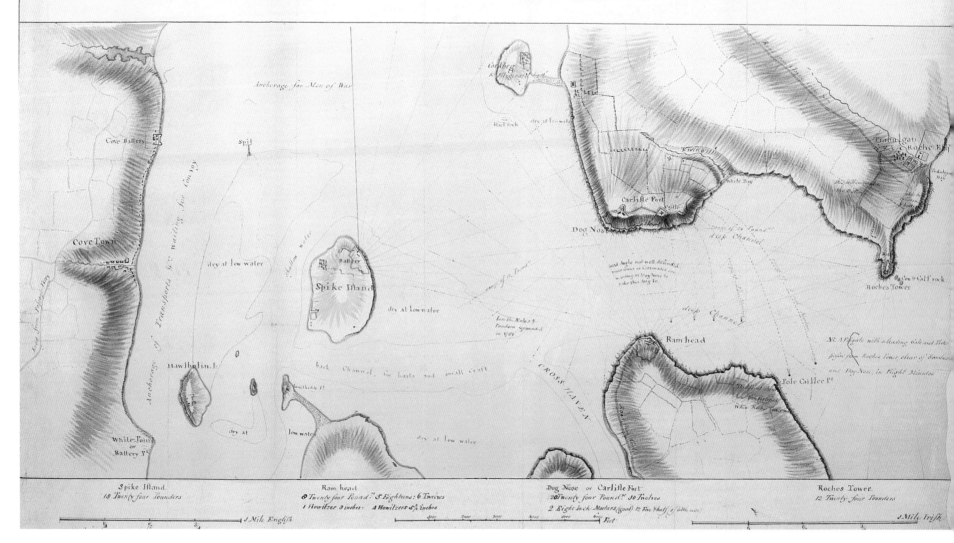

# SURVEY OF THE HARBOUR OF CORKE

from the Entrance to Hawlboling Island: shewing the Ranges of the Batteries constructed for its defence in 1779 and 1781 ——————————————— Cha: Vallancey Lieut Col: Engineer. 1783.

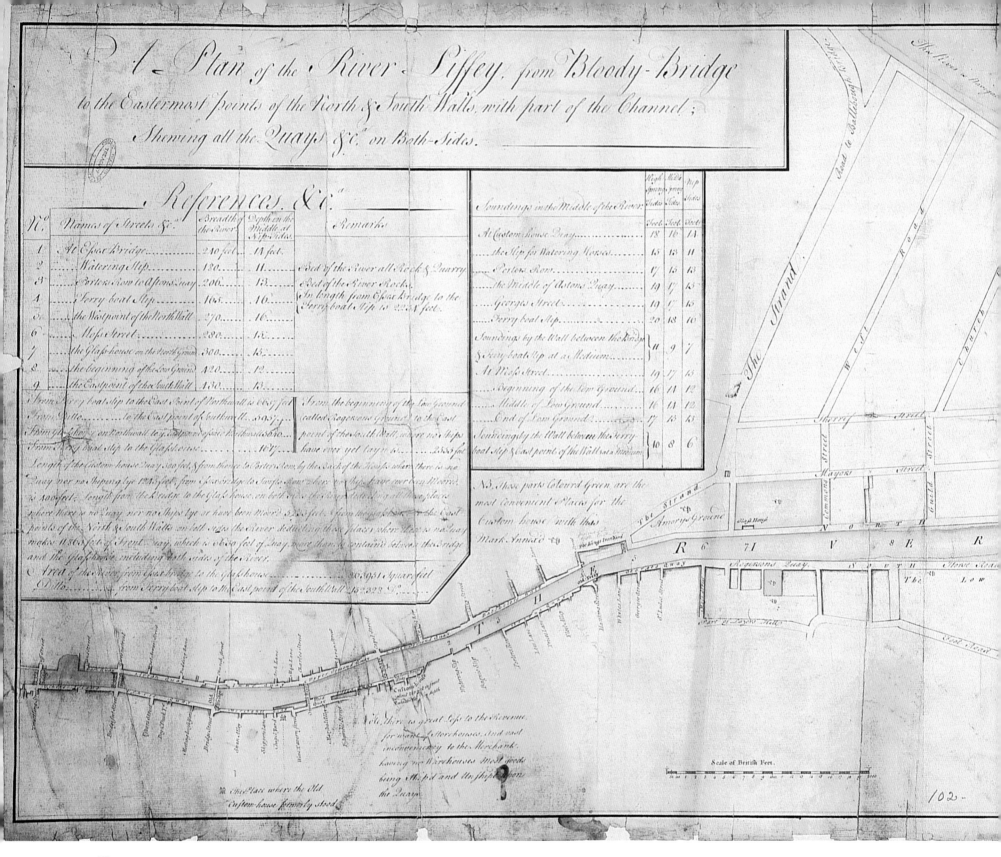

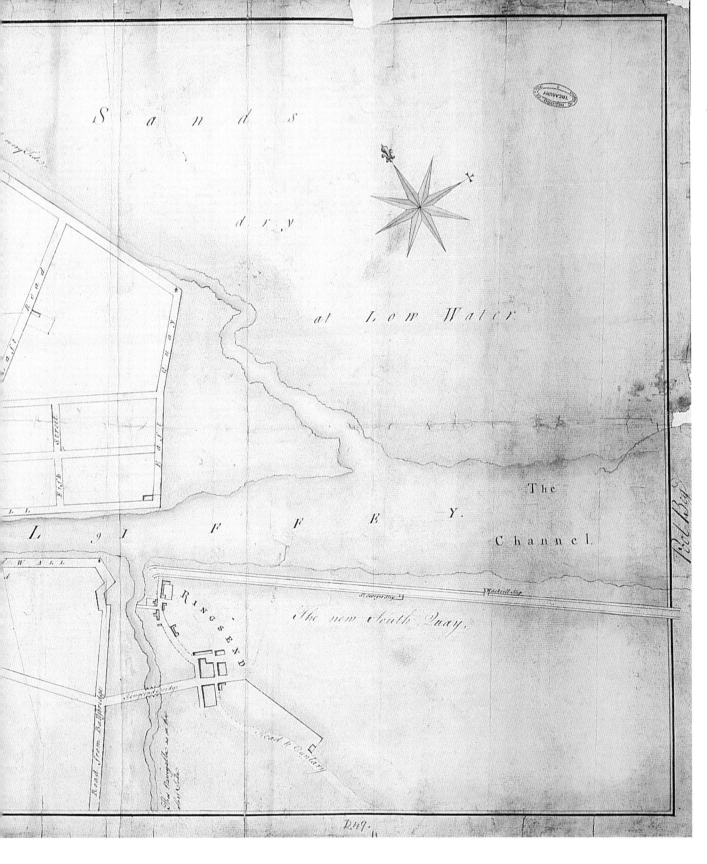

## Dublin c.1790

**Left:** Portraying the River Liffey from Bloody Bridge to the easternmost points of the north and south walls, this map illustrates Dublin as it existed towards the end of the 18th century. Drawn to a scale of 400 feet to one inch, the map also includes reference tables and quays as well as the breadth and depth of the river with soundings at high tide. Dublin was the pivotal point for British rule in Ireland and also the country's principal center for trade.

## Ireland 1793

**Right:** This is described as "A new map of Ireland having the great features of the country described in a manner highly expressive and the distances between the town and stages marked in miles and furlongs for the use of travellers by Alexander Taylor, Lieutenant in his Majesty's Royal Engineers." It shows the state of Ireland towards the end of the 18th century, immediately prior to the Union. The bears a dedication to John, Earl of Westmorland, the then Lord Lieutenant General and Governor General of Ireland. It delineates the various counties of Ireland and indicates the network of roads linking the towns and cities.

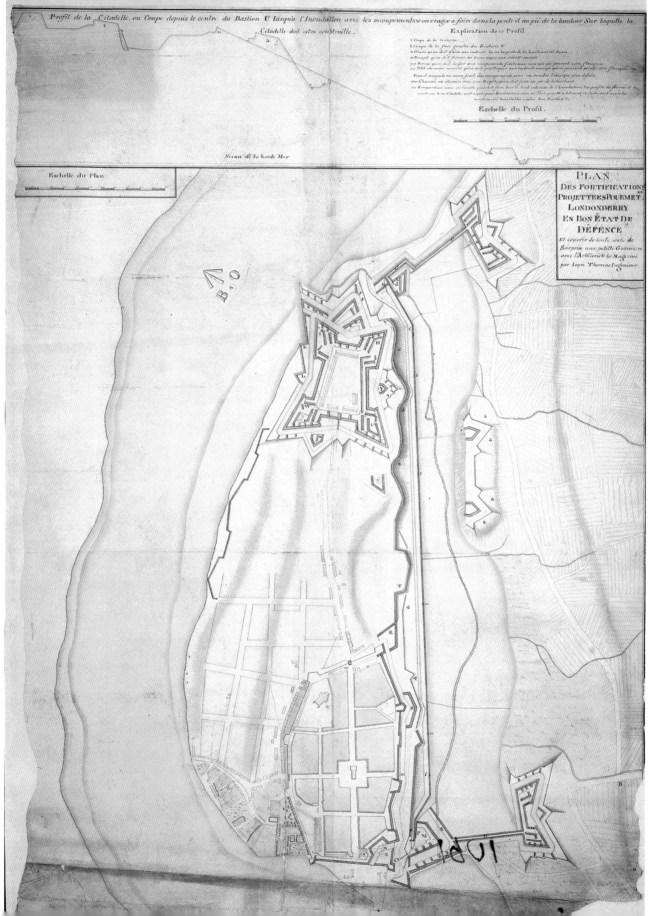

## Londonderry 1799

**Left:** Londonderry (or Derry) is the second city of Northern Ireland and today can lay claim to the finest preserved city walls of any place within the British Isles. This map, produced in French by Jean Thomas and with northeast towards the top, shows the city as it existed at the end of the 18th century along with proposals made for its improved fortification (which were not completed). The city is situated on the River Foyle as it approaches Lough Foyle. The historic core of the city — the Old Town — is shaded red and this is the area surrounded by the early 17th century city walls. Four main streets, mediaeval in origin, meet in a central square, the Diamond. There are four gates in the city walls — Butcher's, Shipquay, Ferryquay and Bishop's. Identifiable at the south side of the old city is St Columb's Cathedral; this is the Protestant cathedral which dates originally from the 17th century (but was altered after the drafting of this map in the 19th century). The origins of the city date back to the 6th century and the foundation of a monastery by Columba the Elder. It was in 1613 that the city was declared a "London Settlement" and thus renamed Londonderry when, as part of the Ulster Plantation, settlers from Scotland and England were encouraged to move to the city by merchants based in London.

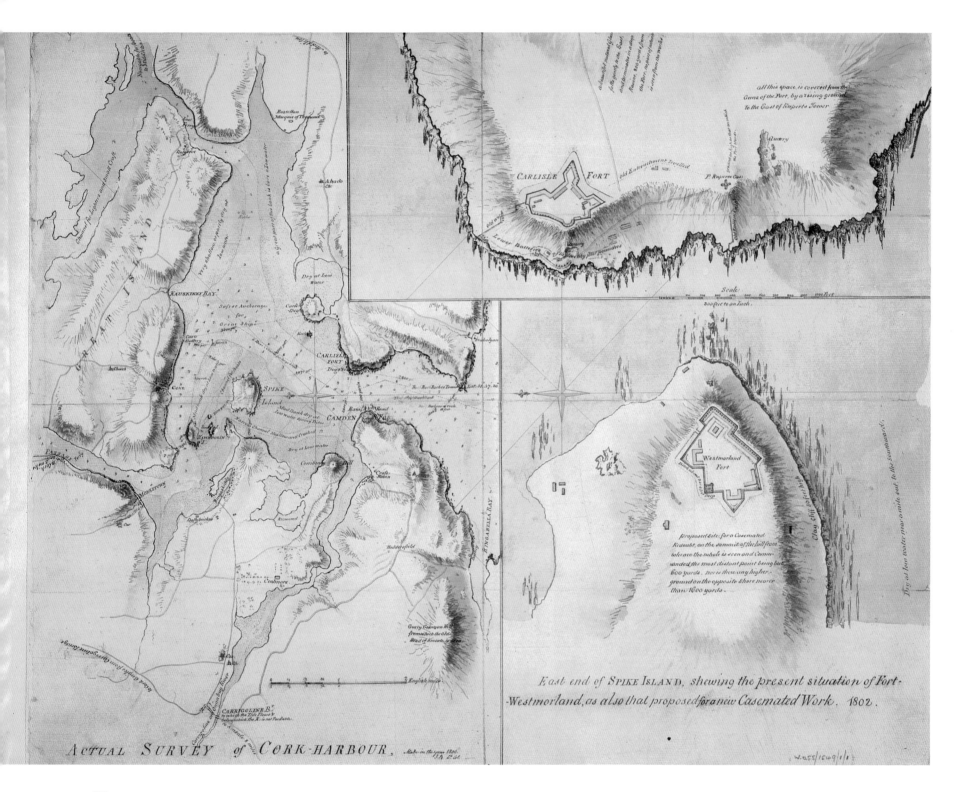

all this space, is covered from the Guns of the Fort, by a rising ground to the East of Ruperts Tower

CARLISLE FORT    old Entrenchment levelled

Quarry

P. Ruperts Cass.

Lower Batteries of of Twenty four Pounders

Scale

500 feet to an Inch

Westmorland Fort

proposed Site: for a Casemated Redoubt, on the summit of the hill from whence the whole is seen and Commanded the most distant point being but 600 yards, nor is there any higher ground on the opposite Shore nearer than 1000 yards.

East end of SPIKE ISLAND, shewing the present situation of Fort-Westmorland, as also that proposed for a new Casemated Work. 1802.

ACTUAL SURVEY of CORK-HARBOUR. Made in the year 1806.

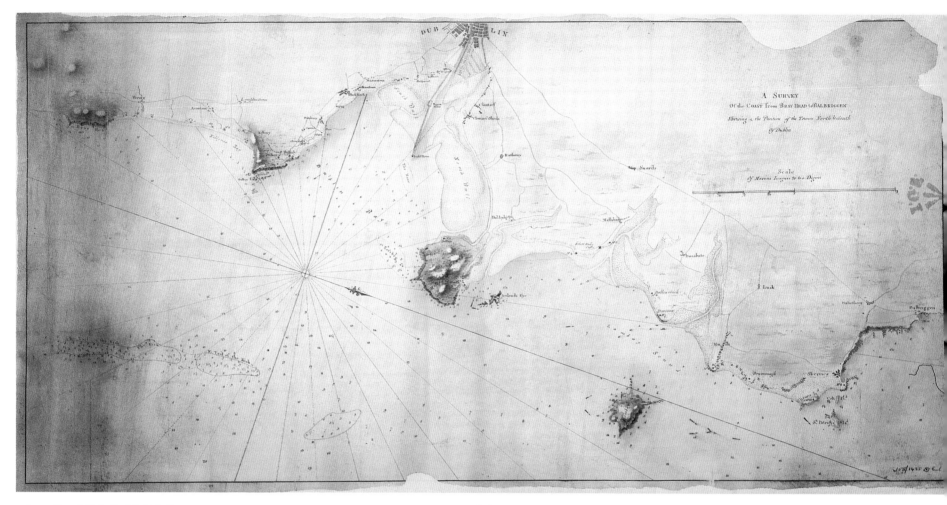

A SURVEY
Of the COAST from BRAY HEAD to BALBRIGGEN

Shewing the Position of the Towers North & South
Of Dublin

Scale
Of Marine Leagues 20 to a Degree

## Cork 1800/1802

**Left:** These three maps illustrate the defensive arrangements to the approaches to Cork Harbor immediately after the French-supported United Irishmen rebellion of 1798. The plan, described as an "Actual Survey of Cork Harbour," is drawn to a scale of about 560 yards to one inch and shows the overall relationship between the defenses and the approaches to the harbor in 1800. The narrowest point of the strait leading into the harbor are defended by Carlisle Fort on the east and Camden Fort to the west — the actual map is aligned with north on the left as indicated by the compass bearing — while the battery on Spike Island to the north forms an additional line of defense for the harbor. The second map, showing Carlisle Fort, was drawn to a scale of 300 feet to one inch and was completed in 1802. Note the references to the former defenses and the location of the lower battery of 20 pounders. Finally, the third map shows Westmorland Fort on Spike Island in 1802 with reference to the proposed construction of a new casemented defensive structure (see the further maps of Spike Island on pages 93 and 106 for a more detailed illustration of this proposed new fortification).

## Dublin c.1800

**Above:** Dating from around the turn of the century, this is a survey of the coast from Brayhead to Balbriggan showing the position of towers north and south of Dublin. Drawn at a scale of quarter of a marine league to one inch, the map also includes soundings. The city of Dublin is located towards the center top of the map, which is aligned (as shown from the compass point) with north towards the bottom right. At a time of war — and this map was drawn at the height of the Napoleonic Wars and shortly after the 1798 rebellion — the chain of coastal towers was an essential link in the defenses of the country. The principle was that each tower was within signaling distance of its neighbor in either direction — remember we are in an age before telegraphic or radio communication — and would therefore be able to form a chain to warn of invasion and thus summon assistance. Inland it was common to see a chain of beacons running from hilltop to hilltop. When speed of message normally relied on man- or horse-power, signals represented the most rapid means of passing information.

## Dublin 1801

**Right and Below Right (detail):** This is a sketch plan of the castle based on a survey in July 1801 by H. Chaigneau and copied by David Robinson in September 1801. The scale is 80 feet to one inch. Dublin Castle is situated on the south side of the River Liffey; from the time of Queen Elizabeth I until the creation of the Irish Free State in 1921, Dublin Castle was the seat of English (and later British) power in Ireland, being the official residence of the Viceroy. Even today, more than 75 years after the creation of the Free State and exactly 50 years after Ireland became a Republic, the Throne Room remains. It is likely that the first castle upon the site dates from the Celtic era, but it was the Vikings whose presence can be established first by archaeological evidence. The Viking castle was replaced by one built on the orders of King John from 1204 until 1226. Much of the site as illustrated here dates from the 18th century and further work was undertaken during the course of the 19th century. The map shows in detail the Upper Yard of the castle and delineates those buildings to the west of this section; note the descriptive key for these buildings. Dublin Castle is still used by the Irish Republic for official functions; when not required for state purposes, the major apartments are open to visitors.

## Cork 1803

**Far Right:** This is a general map of the town and harbor of Cork along with the various islands situated in the approaches to the harbor. It was drawn to accompany Colonel Twiss's report on the defense of Ireland in 1803 by David Robinson following an earlier survey by Lieutenant-Colonel Brown. Westmoreland Fort on Spike Island can be seen to the south of Cove Island whilst the narrowest part of the approaches to the harbor are guarded by forts — called Camden and Carlisle — to the west and east respectively. Further to the west along the coast can be seen Kinsale with Charles ("Chas") Fort guarding the entrance to the harbor. Apart from the actual map, this illustration is also of interest in that it describes the actual provision, both in terms of men and equipment, for each of the defensive points. The history of Cork dates back to the 7th century, when a monastery was built by St Finbarr on an island in the middle of the River Lee. This is where St Finbarr's Cathedral now stands. It became an important fortified base for the Danes and later for the Normans; it was only in 1690 that the city walls were finally dismantled.

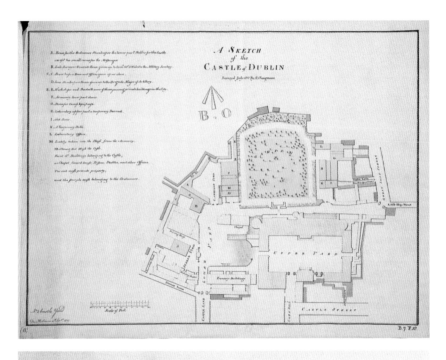

A. House for the Ordnance Storekeeper the lower part Stables for the Castle.
   except two small rooms for the Messengers.

B. Late Surveyor Generals House given up to Lieut. Col. Littlehales the Military Secretary.

C. C. House keepers House and Offices given up as above.

D. Late Storekeepers House given up to the Brigade Major of Artillery.

E. E. Workshops and Shades &c some of them joining private buildings in the City.

F. Armoury. lower part stores.

G. Stores for Camp Equipage.

H. Laboratory. upper part a temporary Barrack.

I. Old Stores.

K. A Temporary Stable.

L. Laboratory Office.

M. Lately taken into the House from the Armoury.

   NB. Strong Red Wash the Castle.

   Faint d.o. Buildings belonging to the Castle,

   as Chapel, Guard house, Prisons, Stables, and other Offices.

   The ink wash private property,

   and the purple wash belonging to the Ordnance.

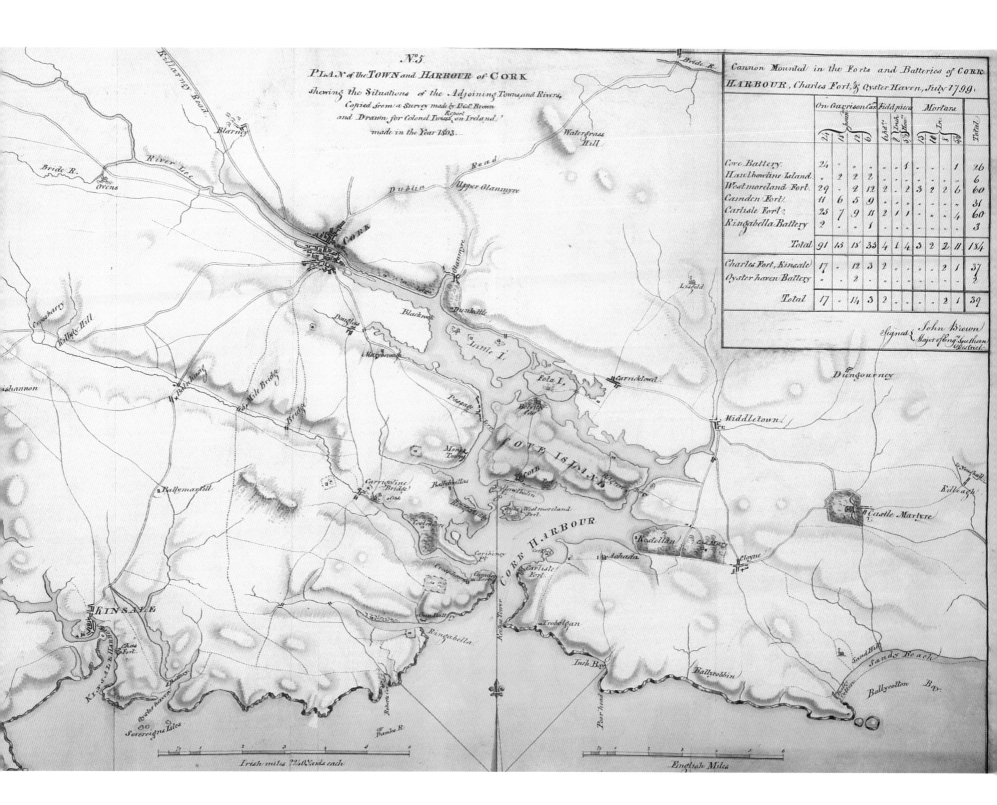

# Dublin 1803

**Below:** Drawn to a scale of about half an inch to one mile, this map illustrates the scale of Dublin during the early years of the 19th century. Showing the relationship between the city, the Grand and Royal Canals, the River Liffey and Phoenix Park, it was one of a number that accompanied Colonel Twiss's report into the defense of Ireland. The map was drawn by W. Chambers and is dated April 30, 1803. Its alignment sees north to the right.

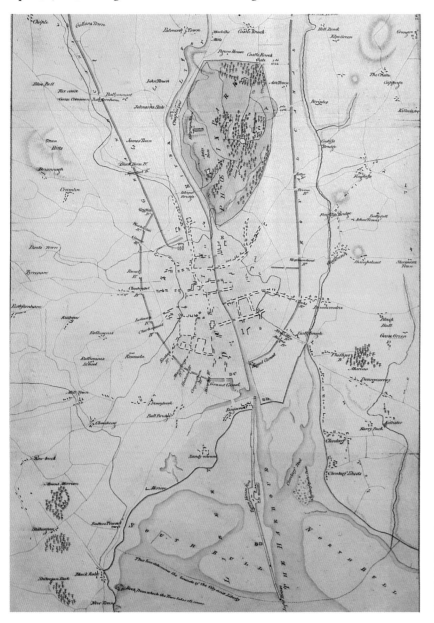

# Dublin 1803

**Below:** This is a general plan of the harbor at Dublin covering the area from Ringsend to the sandbank showing the Pigeon House, drawn to a scale of 500 feet to one inch. The map was sent with Colonel Fisher's letter of August 30, 1803 to Colonel Twiss. This is the easternmost part of the Dublin area and, although subsequently altered, is still recognizable today. The Grand Canal, seen heading southwestwards from the Liffey, circled the south side of Dublin and headed inland, providing access for water-borne traffic to the island's interior. Subsequent changes have included the reclamation of the area described as the South Bull and the construction of extra docks and piers on the north side of the estuary. The Grand Canal, with a length of 80 miles and with 52 locks along its route, provided a link between Dublin Bay and the River Shannon. Construction of the canal began in 1756 and was completed in 1804. Apart from its use for transport, it also improved the water supply to the ever-growing city. The canal's importance declined with the rise of the railways from the mid-19th century. Today the canal is used primarily by leisure craft.

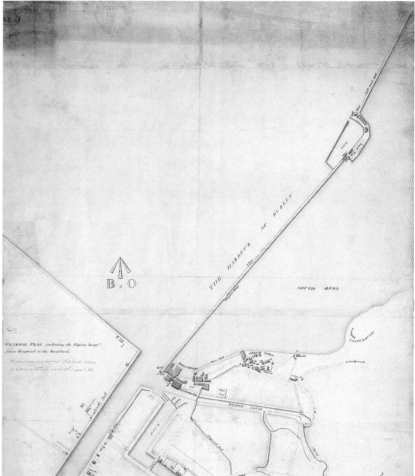

# Dublin 1803

**Below:** This is a sketch map of Dublin complied in 1803. It shows the extent of the city at the time and is drawn to a scale of about 270 yards to one inch. From the map it is possible to identify the King's buildings — highlighted in red — and public buildings — delineated in black. Of the former, most prominent is, inevitably, the castle, while public buildings identified include the Custom House and (Trinity) College. The scale of the city at this stage is evident, with all the built up area well within the Royal Canal to the north and the Grand Canal to the south of the River Liffey. The harbor arrangements are also clearly evident. Dublin experienced rapid growth during the 18th century, with its population expanding from some 65,000 at the start of the century to about 200,000 at the end. The 18th century was also to witness the construction of many of the fine streets, squares and buildings for which the city is still rightly regarded. The classical 18th century buildings include the Bank of Ireland, the Custom House, the Old Library, much of Trinity College (although the college was actually founded in 1592) and Leinster House (home of the Irish parliament). The Royal Canal — 90 miles in length and with 47 locks along its route — provided an alternative, more northerly route, linking Dublin Bay with the River Shannon. Although planned from the 1760s, construction only commenced in 1792 and the route was completed throughout in 1817. The canal was acquired by a railway company and a railway paralleling it was constructed in 1845. Commercially, the canal struggled once the railway revolution arrived. Today the canal, with a preservation groups support, like its southern neighbor is used largely by pleasure craft.

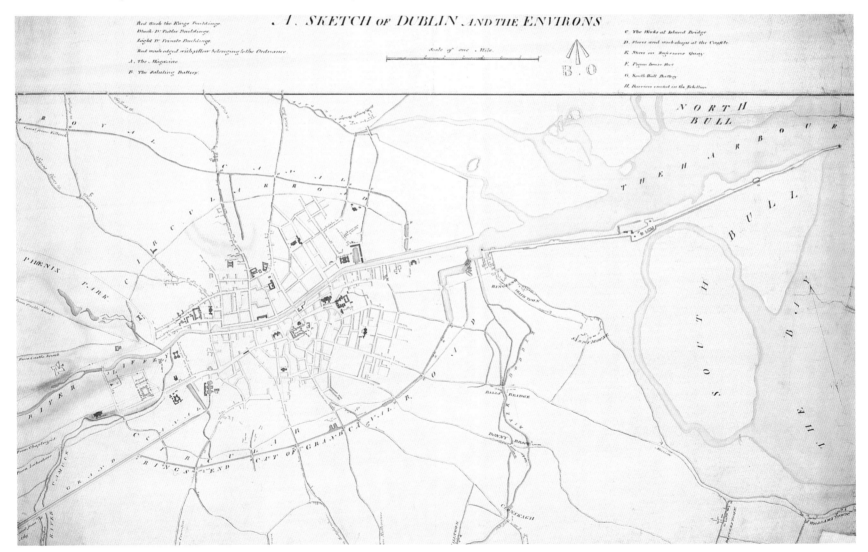

# Enniskillen District 1803

**Below and Right (detail):** The complex network of lakes and waterways in and around Enniskillen, County Fermanagh, is evident in this map of the district drawn by J. Sedley on May 9, 1803. Originally drafted by Captain Taylor in 1797, this map was one of many which accompanied Colonel Twiss's report into the defense of Ireland. It was drawn to a scale of about 550 yards to one inch. The strategic importance of the town of Enniskillen is evident, situated as it is on an island at the east end of Lough Erne, with bridges to the north and south protected by two defensive batteries ("A" and "B"). The accompanying notes refer to the recent establishment of these two batteries and to further defensive works proposed. Fermanagh was one of the original nine counties of the Province of Ulster and one of the six that now form Northern Ireland.

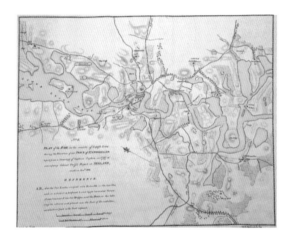

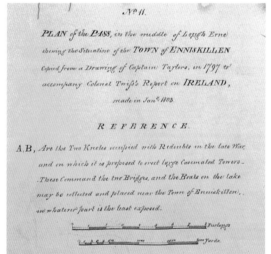

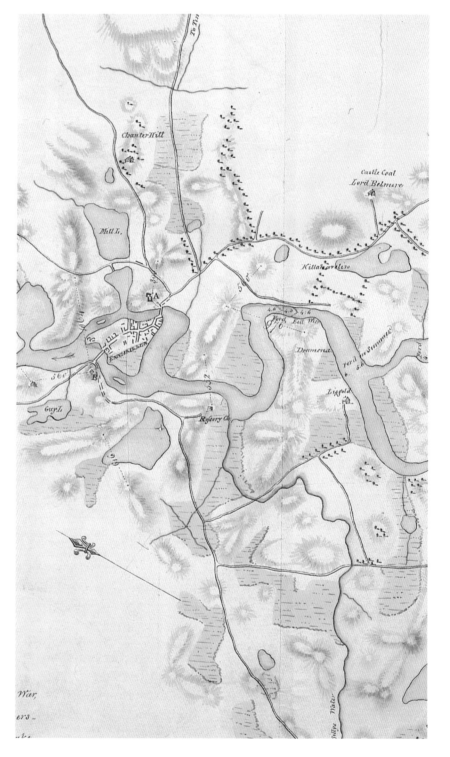

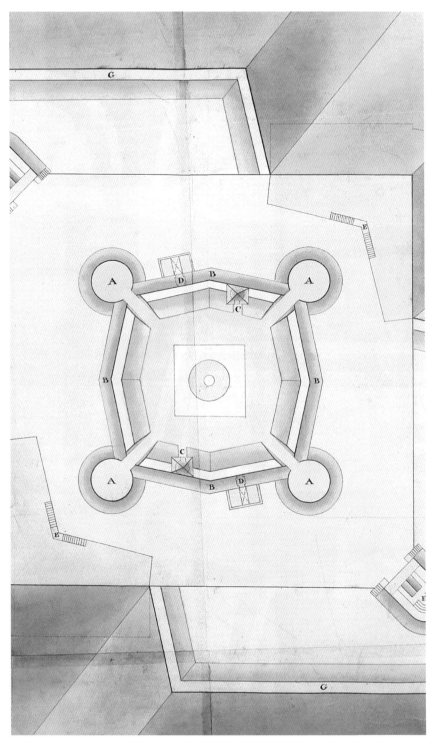

## Ireland 1803

**Below and Right:** The situation in Ireland during the early years of the 19th century was tense. It was only a few years earlier — in 1798 — that a major rising by members of the Society of United Irishmen backed by the French — with whom the British had been at war since 1793 — had led to a serious trouble through much of the island and partial occupation by the French of some of northwest Connacht. The perceived threat, despite the recent Act of Union, was great, particularly as the war against France and Spain continued. In order to counter this threat, much work was undertaken during these years to gauge and, where necessary, improve, the existing defenses. This map, one of a series produced to accompany a report by Colonel Twiss on the defense of Ireland, shows a generic design for a proposed defensive tower to accommodate some 200 to 250 men. Drawn to a scale of 20 feet to one inch, the references are explained in detail in the box at the bottom left.

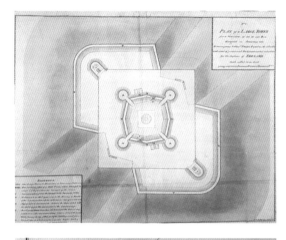

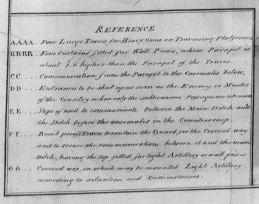

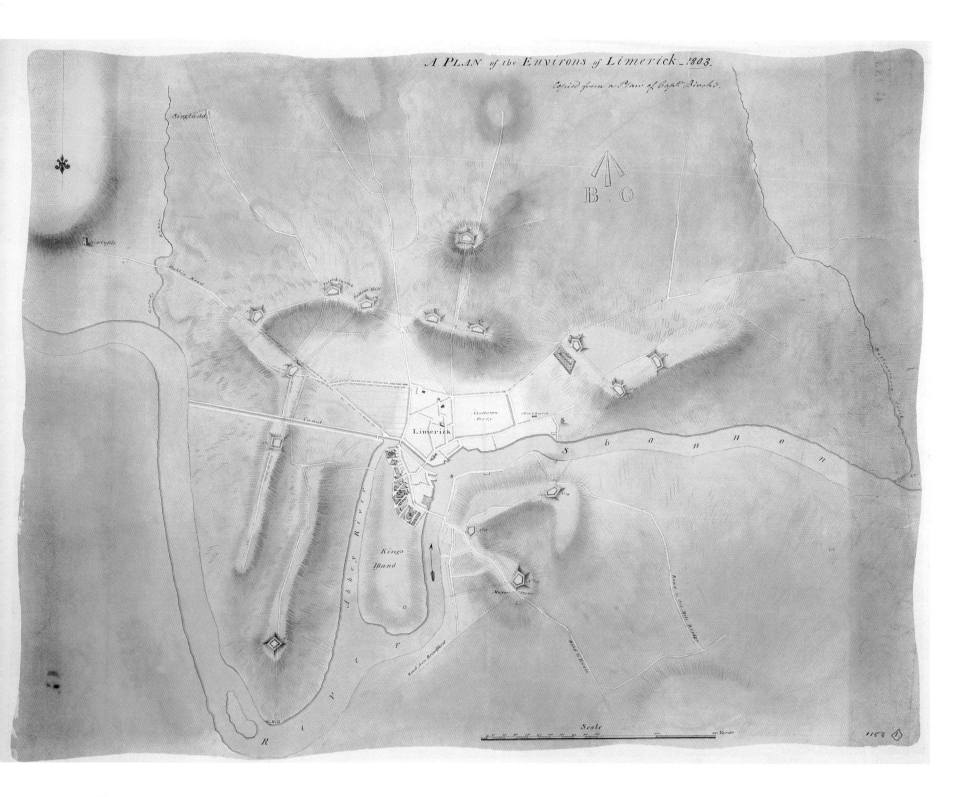

A PLAN of the Environs of Limerick — 1803.

Copied from a Plan of Capt. Birch.

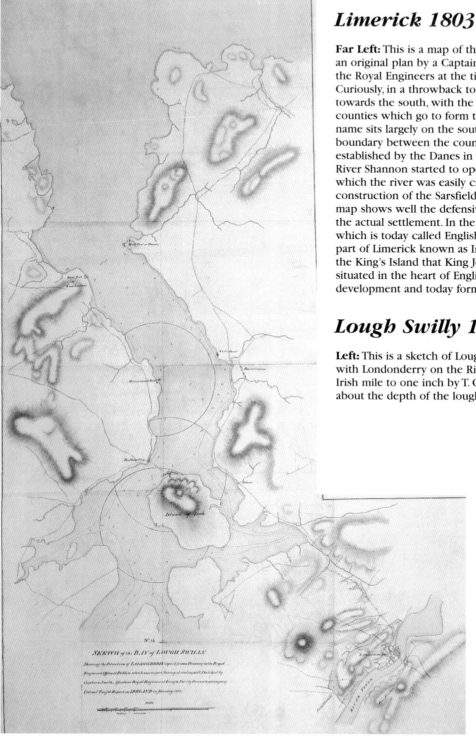

## Limerick 1803

**Far Left:** This is a map of the environs of Limerick in 1803. It was copied from an original plan by a Captain Birch — possibly J. F. Birch who was a Captain in the Royal Engineers at the time — and is scaled at about 300 yards to the inch. Curiously, in a throwback to earlier maps, the top of the illustration is in fact towards the south, with the north towards the bottom. Limerick is one of the six counties which go to form the province of Munster and the town of the same name sits largely on the south bank of the River Shannon; the river forms the boundary between the counties of Limerick and Clare. The town of Limerick was established by the Danes in the 9th century and it marked the point where the River Shannon started to open up into the estuary and was, thus, the last point at which the river was easily crossed by ford. The date of this map predates the construction of the Sarsfield Bridge (1824-35) across the River Shannon. The map shows well the defensive arrangements for the town as well as the scale of the actual settlement. In the center is King's Island; this is the part of Limerick which is today called English Town. Across the Abbey River, to the south, is that part of Limerick known as Irish Town and beyond that Newtown Perry. It was on the King's Island that King John had his castle built. St Mary's Cathedral is also situated in the heart of English Town. Newtown Pery was an 18th century development and today forms the commercial center of Limerick.

## Lough Swilly 1803

**Left:** This is a sketch of Lough Swilly in County Donegal showing its relationship with Londonderry on the River Foyle. The map was copied to the scale of half an Irish mile to one inch by T. Crompton on April 30, 1803. Information is also given about the depth of the lough at various points.

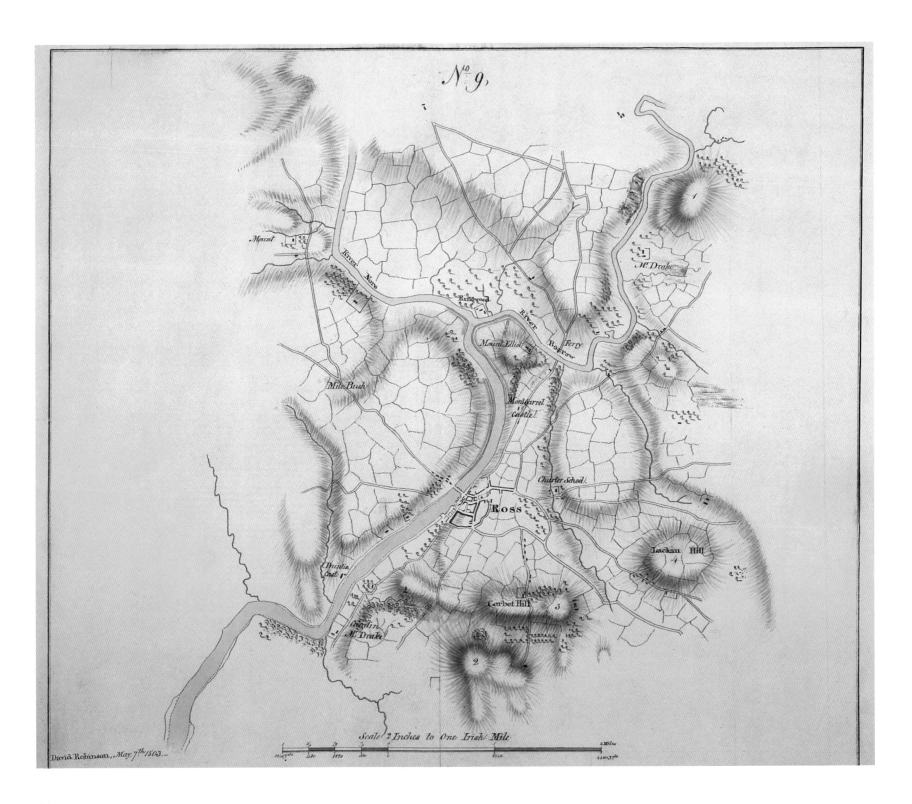

Mount

River Nore

Ringwood

M.ᶜ Drake

River Barrow

Mount Elliott

Ross Ferry

Mile Bush

Mountgarret Castle.

Charter School.

**Ross**

Dunda Cast.

Lackan Hill

Corbet Hill

Garden M.ᶜ Drake

Scale 2 Inches to One Irish Mile

David Robinson, May 7.ᵗʰ 1803.—

# New Ross 1803

**Left:** Located in County Wexford, the most southeasterly of the Province of Leinster, New Ross is situated on the River Barrow about half way between Waterford and Wexford. This map shows the township and surrounding district. It was drawn to a scale of half an Irish mile to one inch by David Robinson on May 7, 1803 and is, again, one of the documents accompanying Colonel Twiss's report into the defense of Ireland. At the time, as today, New Ross was the most southerly point at which it was possible to cross the River Barrow by road and was, therefore, of considerable importance in the defense of this corner of Ireland.

# Spike Island 1803

**Below:** Spike Island, in the approaches to Cork, was one of major strategic importance to the defense of the harbor and town. Drawn by T. Crompton on April 21, 1803, this map was one of a number that accompanied Colonel Twiss's report on the defense of Ireland. It shows the existing Westmoreland Fort as well as the site of a proposed new establishment.

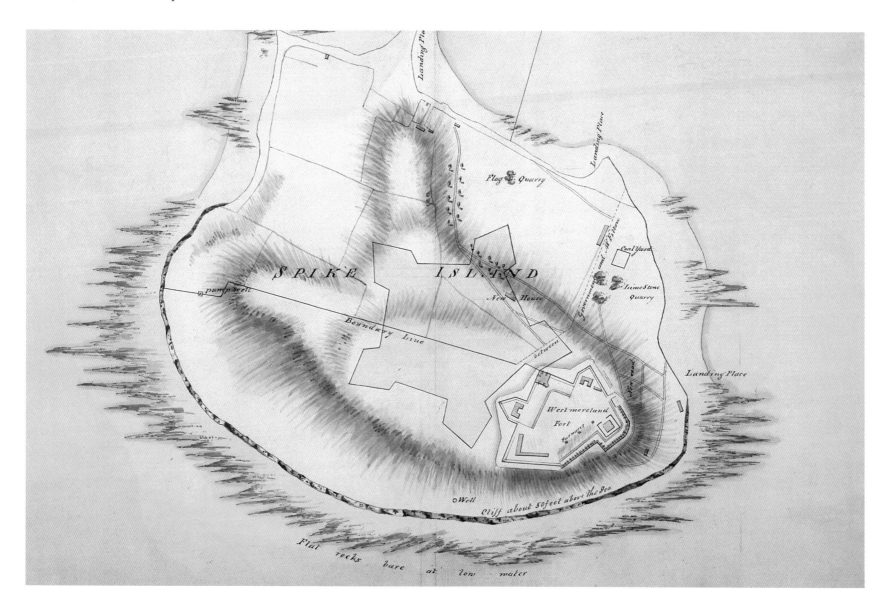

# Ireland 1804

**Right and details:** Described as a "New Map of Ireland ... for the use of Travellers," this map was compiled originally by Alexander Taylor, a Lieutenant in the Royal Engineers and originally published by William Faden in 1793 and then again in 1804 with revisions. It is dedicated to the Earl of Westmorland, Lord Lieutenant General and Governor-General, in a decorative cartouche that is supported on the left by Britannia and on the right by a figure representing Justice. Although a commercially produced map, this example is of considerable additional interest for the alterations made in manuscript pointing out the defensive arrangements around the coast. A key, at the top right (see details), describes in detail the various military establishments — both actual and proposed — demonstrating the considerable importance that was attached to the defense of Ireland at a time of threat from the French forces under Napoleon. When the map was compiled, it was only a few years since the French had supported an attempted rebellion by Irish nationalists. So the threat that these defensive stations were designed to counter was very real.

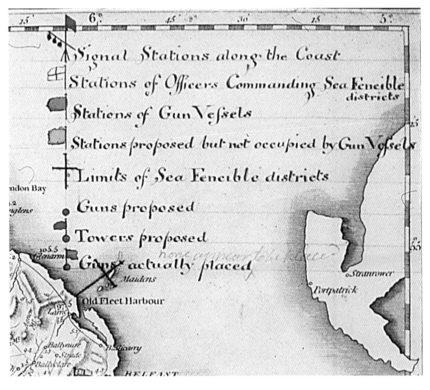

Signal Stations along the Coast

Stations of Officers Commanding Sea Fencible districts

Stations of Gun Vessels

Stations proposed but not occupied by Gun Vessels

Limits of Sea Fencible districts

Guns proposed

Towers proposed

Guns actually placed

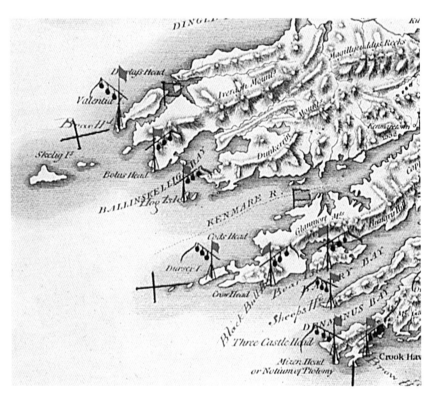

## Cork 1809

**Below:** Dated May 1, 1809 and signed by Lieutenant-Colonel W. Fenwick, this map shows progress on the new fort on Spike Island in the approaches to Cork harbor. It shows a plan and section of the new works and was drawn to a scale of 50 feet to one inch by Lieutenant G. O. Watson of the Royal Engineers. As one of the most important harbors in Ireland, Cork was inevitably a potential military target during the French Wars of 1793 to 1815 and these additional defenses were designed to counter this perceived threat.

## Ballincollig 1810

**Right:** Ballincollig is situated some five miles west of Cork along the River Lee. At the time that this map was drafted Britain was still at war with Napoleon's France. Ireland, while nominally now a single state with the rest of the United Kingdom, following the Act of Union, was still a potential source of trouble. Periods of war and civil strife inevitably saw the construction of enhanced facilities. The map is one of a series illustrating a proposed Artillery Establishment at Ballincollig and it shows, at a scale of about 270 feet to one inch, a plan of all the Royal Gunpowder Mills and their relationship to the proposed Artillery Establishment.

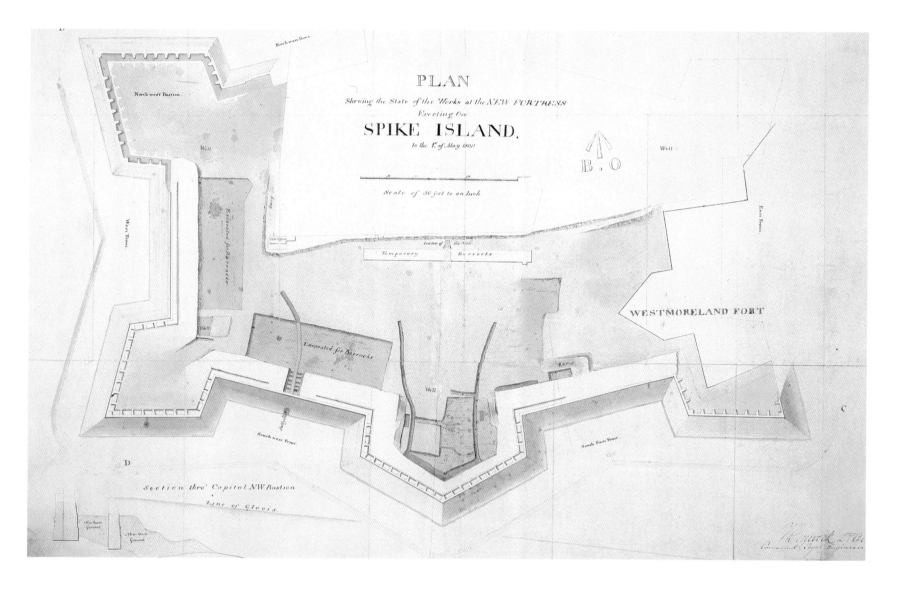

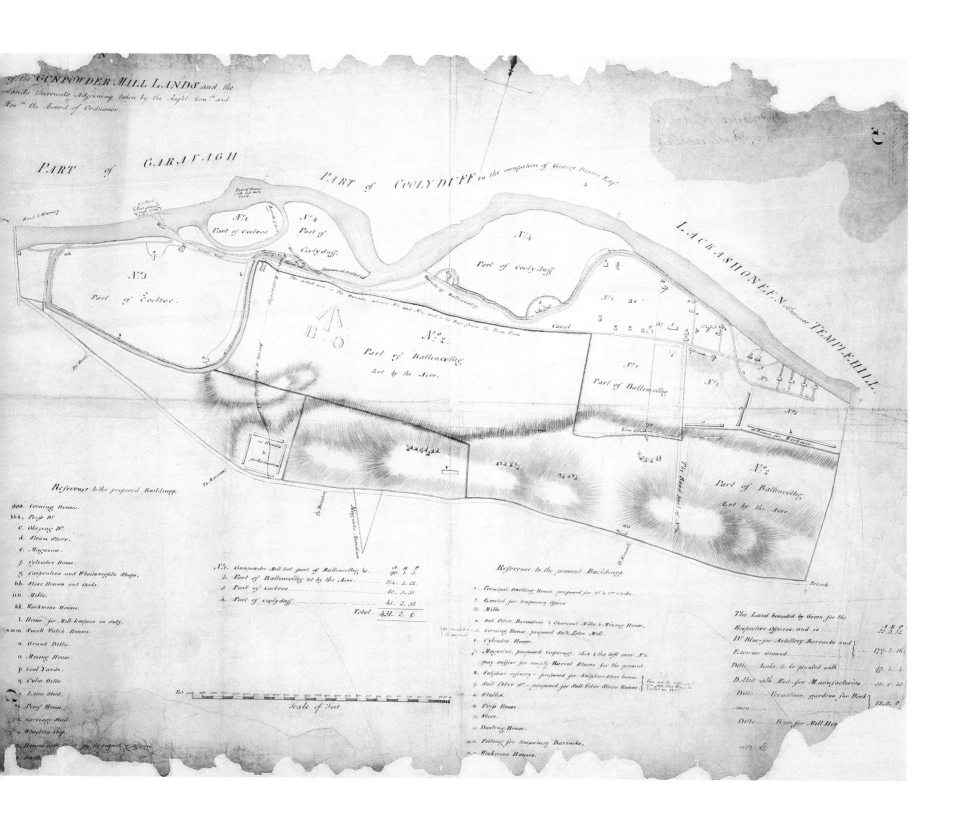

of the *GUNPOWDER MILL LANDS* and the
Lands thereunto Adjoining taken by the Right Hon.ble and
Hon.ble the Board of Ordnance.

PART of GARAVAGH

PART of COOLYDUFF in the occupation of George Davies Esq.r

LACHASHONEEN otherwise TEMPLEHILL.

No 1.
Part of Coolroe

No 4
Part of
Cooly duff.

No 4
Part of Cooly duff

No 3
Part of Coolroe.

B O

No 2
Part of Ballincollig

Let by the Acre.

No 5

No 1
Part of Ballincollig

No 1

No 2

Canal

Lime Kiln

No 2
Part of Ballincollig

Let by the Acre.

To Cork

**Reference to the proposed Buildings.**

a.a.a. Corning Houses.
b.b.b. Press D.o
c. Glazing D.o
d. Steam Store.
e. Magazine.
f. Cylinder House.
g. Carpenters and Wheelwrights Shops.
h.h. Store Houses and sheds.
i.i.i.i. Mills.
k.k. Workmens Houses.
l. House for Mill-keepers on duty.
m.m.m. Small Watch Houses.
n. Grand Ditto.
o. Mixing House.
p. Coal Yards.
q. Culm Ditto.
r. Lime Shed.
s. Proof House.
t. Carriage Shed.
u. Wheelers Shop.
x. Houses and for the respecte Officers.
y. Smith.

No 1. Gunpowder Mill Let part of Ballincollig &c. ... 90. 1. 3.
2. Part of Ballincollig let by the Acre ... 214. 2. 22.
3. Part of Coolroe ... 83. 3. 33.
4. Part of Cooly duff ... 43. 2. 32.
                                    Total. 431. 2. 6

Scale of Feet.

**Reference to the present Buildings.**

1. Principal Dwelling House proposed for 1.st & 2.d Clerks.
2. Erected for temporary Officers.
3. Mills.
4. Salt Petre, Brimstone & Charcoal Mills & Mixing House.
5. Corning House, proposed Salt Petre Mill.
6. Cylinder House.
7. Magazine, proposed Cooperage, this & the loft over No 5 may suffice for empty Barrel Stores for the present.
8. Sulphur refinery - proposed for Sulphur Store house.
9. Salt Petre d.o - proposed for Salt Petre Store House.
10. Stables.
11. Press House.
12. Store.
13. Dusting House.
14. Fitting for temporary Barracks,
15. Workmens Houses.

The Land bounded by Green for the
Respective Officers, and is ... 22. 3. 32
D.o Blue - for Artillery Barracks and
Exercise Ground ... 179. 3. 26
Ditto Lake, to be planted with ... 27. 1. 4.
Dotted with Red for Manufactories. 55. 0. 35
Ditto Vermillion, gardens for Work-
men. ... 55. 2. 0.
Ditto Blue for Mill Ho.

97

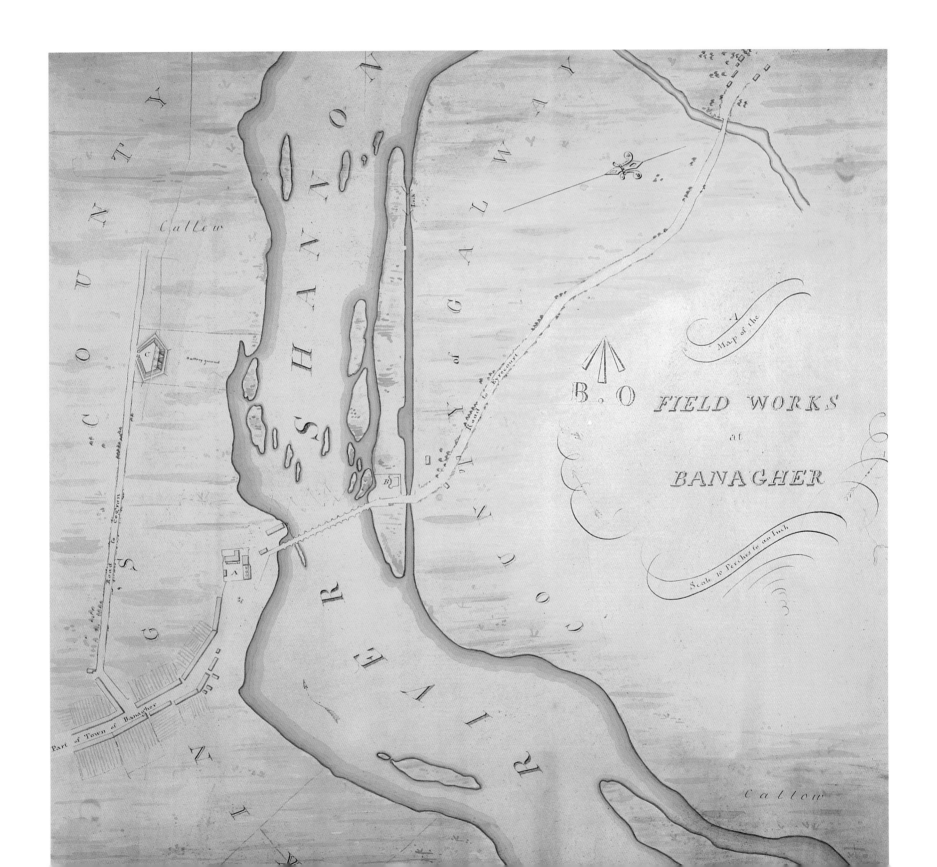

Map of the

FIELD WORKS
at
BANAGHER

Scale 10 Perches to an Inch

## Banagher 1810

**Left:** Today known as County Offaly in the Province of Leinster, under British rule the area was known as King's County. Banagher is a settlement located on the east bank of the River Shannon, which at this point forms the boundary with the Province of Connacht. There is a bridge across the river at the same point and, therefore, the location was of strategic importance. This map, which accompanied a letter dispatched by Brigadier-General Fisher of May 23, 1810, was drawn by C. Mann to a scale of ten perches to one inch. It shows the fieldworks — ie the defenses — located at Banagher during the last years of the Napoleonic Wars. King's County was one of the plantations established after the Ulster Plantations, in this case in 1620. Its land ownership was to be further altered when, after Cromwell's campaign, a whole swathe of land (from Antrim in the north to Waterford in the south, plus a one-mile coastal strip around Connacht) was granted to veterans of the Parliamentary Army.

## Hollymount 1810

**Below:** This highly detailed map shows the parish of Hollymount with the town and harbor of Westport — Cathair na Mart — in County Mayo. The original was drawn by Henry Browne of the Royal Sappers and Miners. The town is situated at the southeast point of Clew Bay at the point in which the River Carrowbeg flows into Westport Bay. As can be seen from the nature of the town plan, Westport was a planned settlement; it was designed, possibly by a French architect, and founded by the Earl of Altamont in 1780. Its primary purpose was to act as a port, but this importance declined with the arrival of the railways. Today the town — widely regarded as one of the most attractive in Ireland — is a center for anglers. Westport House, visible to the east of White Lough (the map, it should be noted sees north toward the right) was originally built by Richard Cassels in the early 1730s and later extended by James Wyatt. The house, one of the finest stately homes in Ireland, is the ancestral home of the Marquess of Sligo.

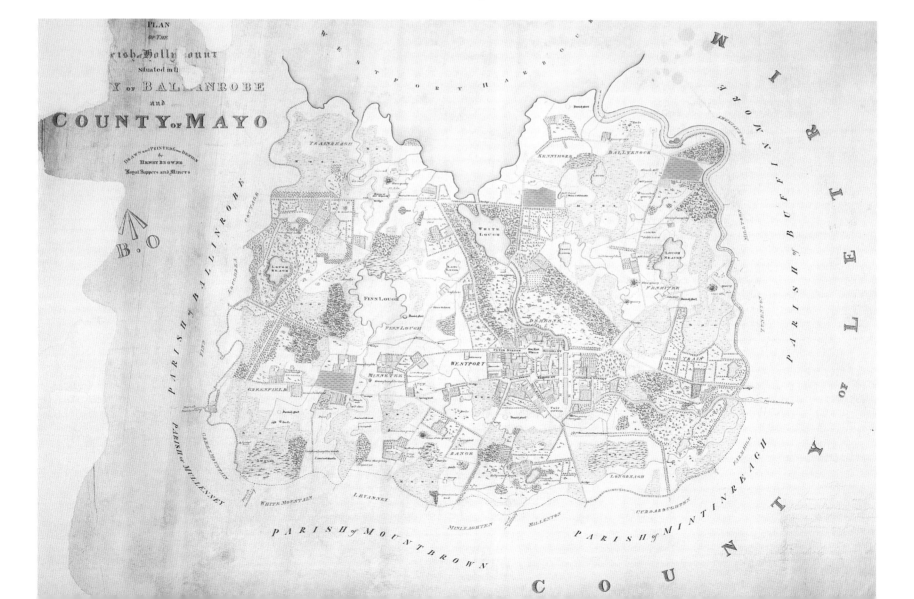

## Ireland 1810

**Right:** This is an outline map of Ireland compiled in November 1810 at the time of the Napoleonic war almost a decade after the Act of Union. It is of particular interest in that it shows the disposition of the British forces in Ireland at the time. The key indicates the status of each of these military establishments. Also shown, alongside each of the base in red, is the distance from Dublin. It should be noted that the heaviest military presence is around the coast. This was inevitable, given that the country had suffered from French and rebel landings since the outbreak of the war against France in 1793. Inland, reflecting the fact that in an era before road and railway travel existed water was the primary form of transport, other bases are adjacent to canals and rivers.

# *Meelick 1810*

**Below:** Located in County Galway, in the Province of Connacht, Meelick was, like Banagher shown on page 98, on the River Shannon and is slightly south of Banagher. At 230 miles in length, the Shannon (with its associated lakes) is the longest river in Ireland and is today a popular venue for long distance river cruises. This map is another which accompanied the letter sent by Brigadier-General Fisher on May 23, 1810. Like that of Banagher, it was drawn by C. Mann, although this time the scale is about 20 perches to one inch. The map shows the defensive works at this location and across the River Shannon in King's County.

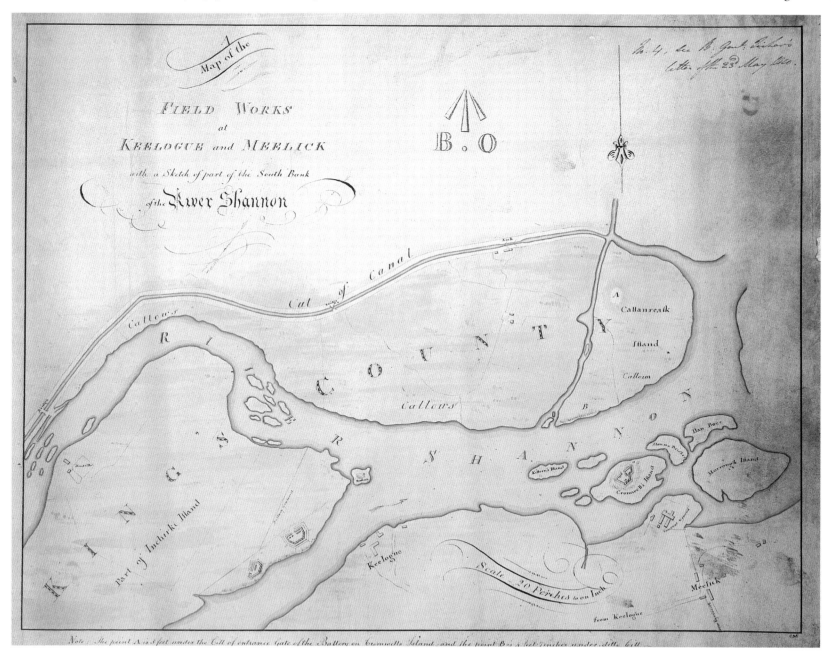

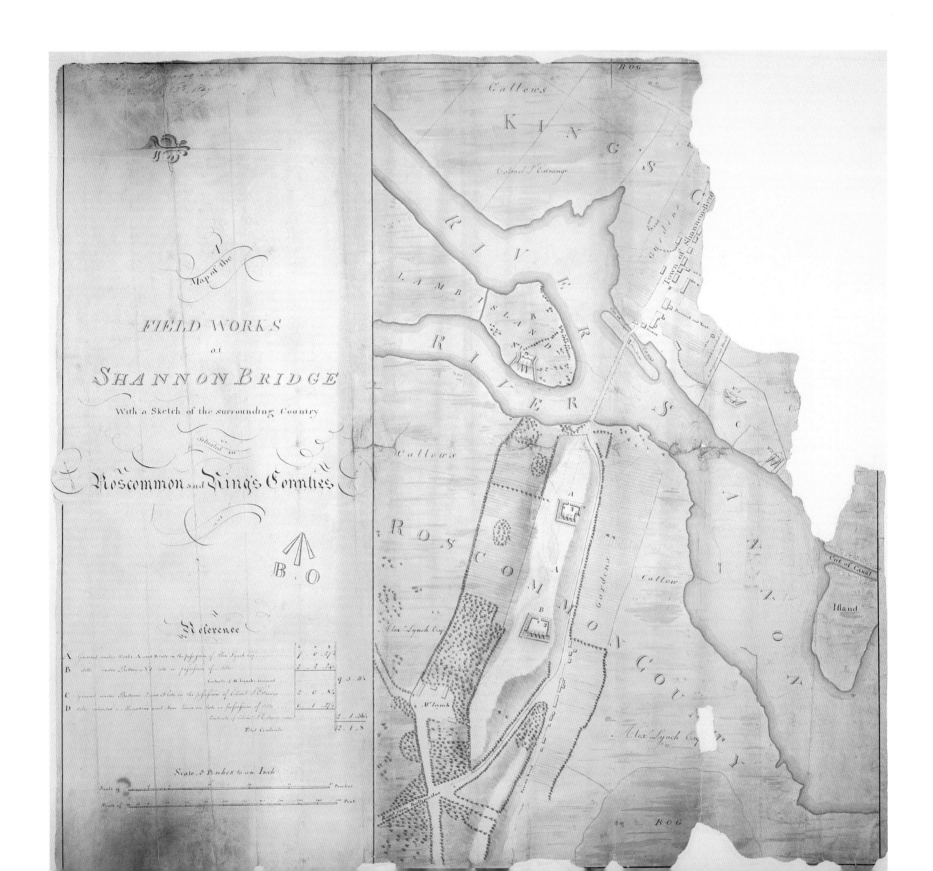

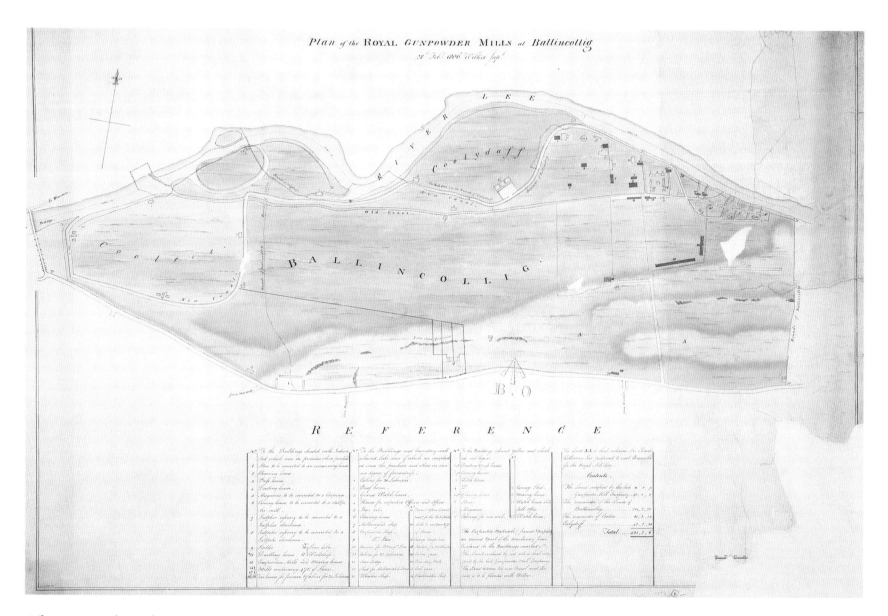

## Shannonbridge 1810

**Left:** Drawn to a scale of around 170 feet to one inch, this map shows the field-works — ie defensive works — at Shannonbridge located between Roscommon and King's County (Offaly). The River Shannon marks the boundary between the provinces of Connacht and Leinster. Shannonbridge is located just to the south of Athlone and, as its name implies, was one of the few locations where the river could be crossed. The bridge illustrated in the map still stands to this day. River crossings had great strategic importance in this period and so were always included on military maps of the time.

## Ballincollig 1811

**Above:** Originally drafted in 1806, this version of the map was copied in 1811 by S. B. Howlett. It shows a plan of the Royal Gunpowder Mills at Ballincollig and can be compared with the earlier map on page 97. Dated February 28, 1806, this map was drawn by C. Wilks and is scaled at about 250 feet to one inch. The manufacture of gunpowder, which is comprised of saltpeter, sulfur and charcoal, was an essential part of the British military establishment both on the mainland and in Ireland; naval dockyards and ordnance works were constructed in many parts of the British Isles, such as Portsmouth, Plymouth and Chatham.

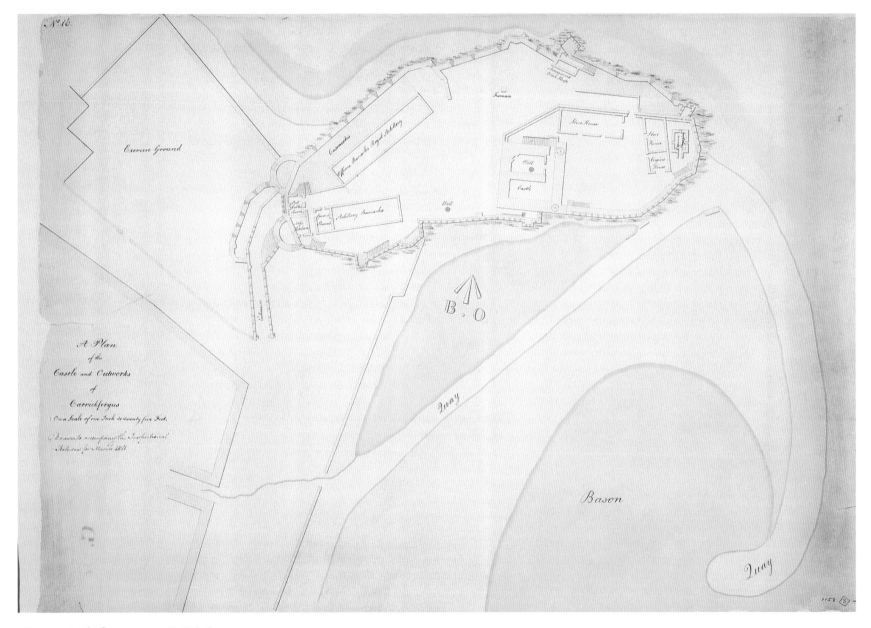

# Carrickfergus 1811

**Above:** The history of Carrickfergus Castle has already been described on page page 48, but by the late 18th century, following capture by the French in 1760 (the last time it was occupied by enemy forces), it had become a prison. Following this, it reverted to a military use during the French wars of 1793-1815, when its defenses were strengthened and it became primarily an arsenal. It retained a military role through until 1928. This map, drawn to a scale of 25 feet to one inch, was copied by Robert Hoddle and accompanied the Inspection Report of March 1811, having been endorsed by Colonel Fisher. The castle's position on a rocky promontory on the north side of Belfast Lough is clearly evident. Note also the references to the quays; Carrickfergus was, until the rise to prominence of Belfast, an important harbor.

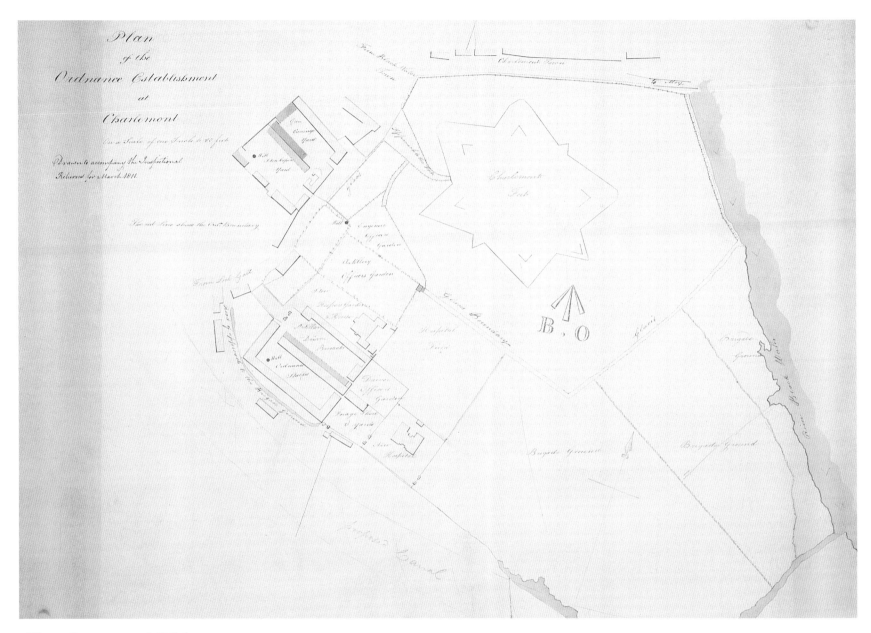

# Charlemont 1811

**Above:** Described as a "Plan of the Ordnance Establishment at Charlemont," this illustration shows the arrangement at Charlemont in County Armagh. Drawn to a scale of eight feet to one inch, the map was copied by M. Wolfe and accompanied the Inspectional Report of March 1811. Charlemont is located about seven miles north of Armagh and is situated on the southside of the Blackwater; the river forms the boundary between Counties Tyrone and Armagh. Charlemont Castle was the scene of one of the most dramatic actions in the period prior to the onset of the English Civil War in 1642. On October 22, 1641, the castle was seized by a group of native Ulsterman, led by Sir Phelim O'Neill. These rebels claimed to be acting on the King's behalf against "evil counsellors," but their action precipitated war in Ireland which, ultimately, led to the arrival of Cromwell's army at the end of that decade.

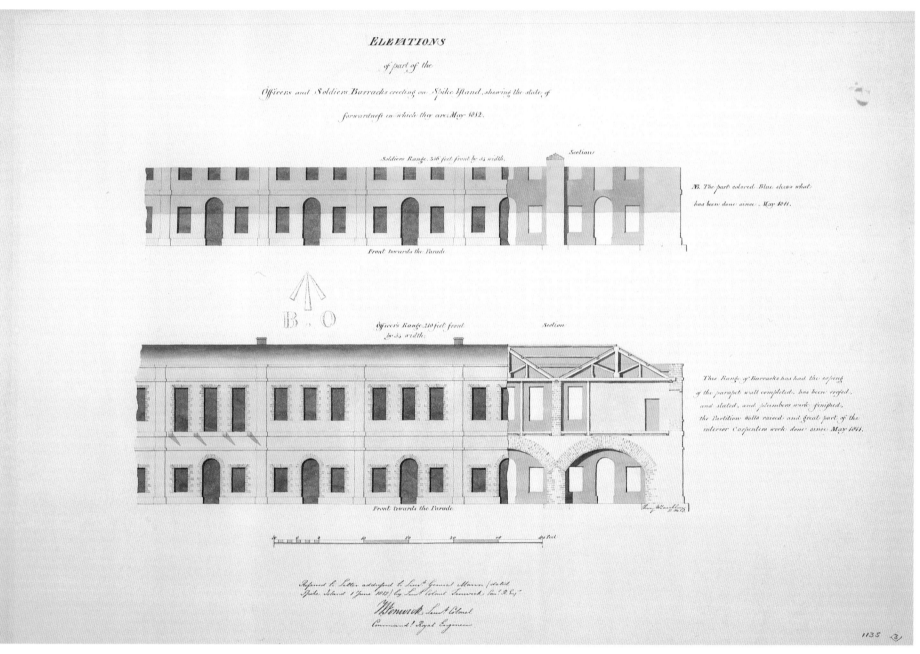

## Cork 1812

**Above:** Another illustration portraying the defenses on Spike Island in the approaches to Cork harbor (see also pages 83 and 93). The drawings are signed by Lieutenant-Colonel Fenwick of the Royal Engineers and are referred to in his letter to Lieutenant-General Mann dated June 1, 1812. To a scale of eight feet to one inch, the drawings illustrate the elevations of part of the officers' and soldiers' barracks being erected on Spike Island, showing the progress made by May 1812.

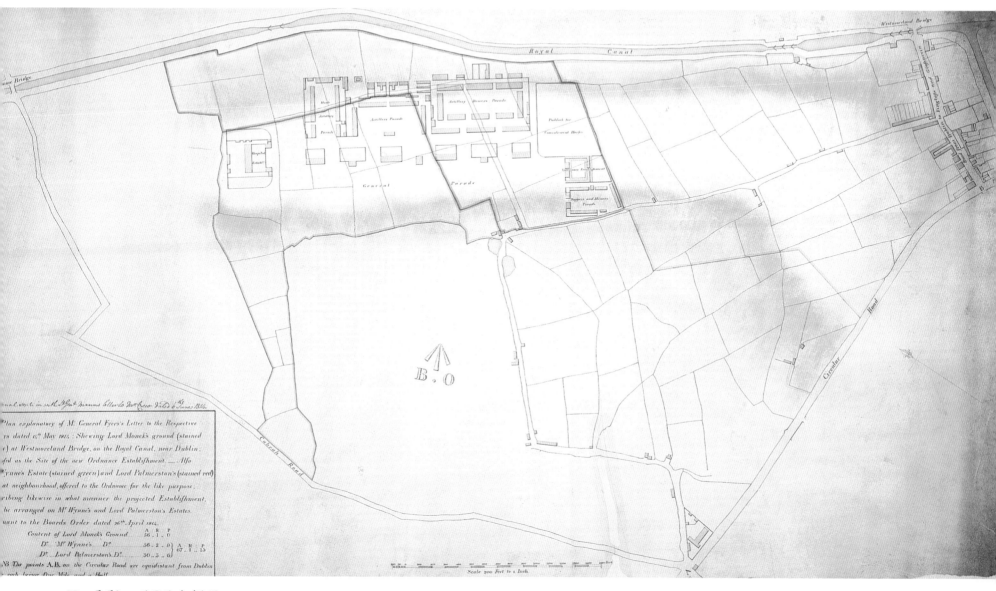

## Dublin 1814/15

**Above:** Located on the southeast side of Dublin, Westmoreland Bridge is one of a number of crossings over the Grand Canal. This map shows the site of a proposed new Ordnance Establishment adjacent to the bridge and was an explanatory plan to accompany documentation sent by Major-General Fyer on May 14, 1814. The land that would be occupied by the proposed development belonged to three individuals — Lord Monck (marked in yellow), Mr Wynne (green) and Lord Palmerston (red). The map illustrates how sparsely developed this area was at the time and was drawn to a scale of 200 feet to one inch. Lord Palmerston was one of the most influential political figures of 19th century British history. Born in 1784, he succeeded to the Irish Viscountcy in 1802, becoming a Tory MP in 1807; he was to become a Whig in 1829. He sat in the House of Commons for 58 years, until his death in 1865, holding ministerial office for 48 years of which 38 years were spent in the Cabinet. He was Secretary of War 1809-28, Foreign Secretary 1830-41 and 1846-51, Home Secretary 1852-55 and Prime Minister 1855-58, and again 1859-65, when he died in office.

## Charlemont 1815

**Right:** This map, drawn to a scale of
40 feet to one inch, shows that part of
the town and borough of Charlemont
in Armagh demised to the Ordnance
Department. Apart from portraying the
land owned by the Ordnance, adjacent
land ownership is also indicated. The
map was surveyed by Thomas
Donnelly in 1815.

## Kinsale 1815

**Far Right:** Copied by C. Bassett, 2nd
Class RMSD, on February 24, 1815, this
map shows the Ordnance land at
Charles Fort, Kinsale, at the end of the
Napeolonic Wars. Drawn to a scale of
100 feet to one inch, the map shows
clearly the military establishment at
this point after some 20 years of
European war. The original star-shaped
Charles Fort — named after the Stuart
King Charles II — was built in 1677;
the well-preserved fortifications are
still an impressive sight. The barracks,
dating from the 19th century, are
ruined today, but are still accessible
to visitors. Kinsale was an important
strategic point guarding the approaches to Cork and a second fort — James
Fort (named after King James II) — is
on the opposite side of the inlet.

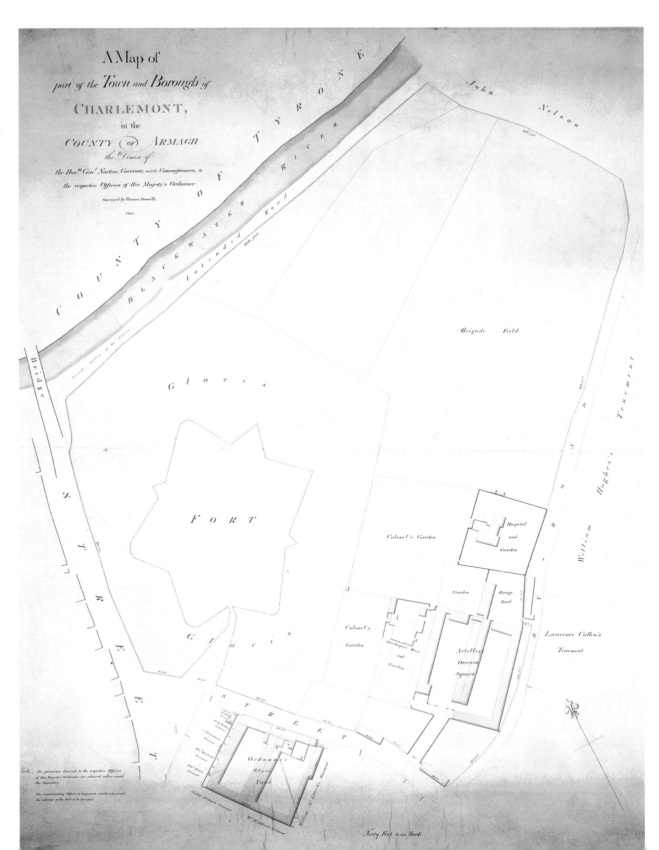

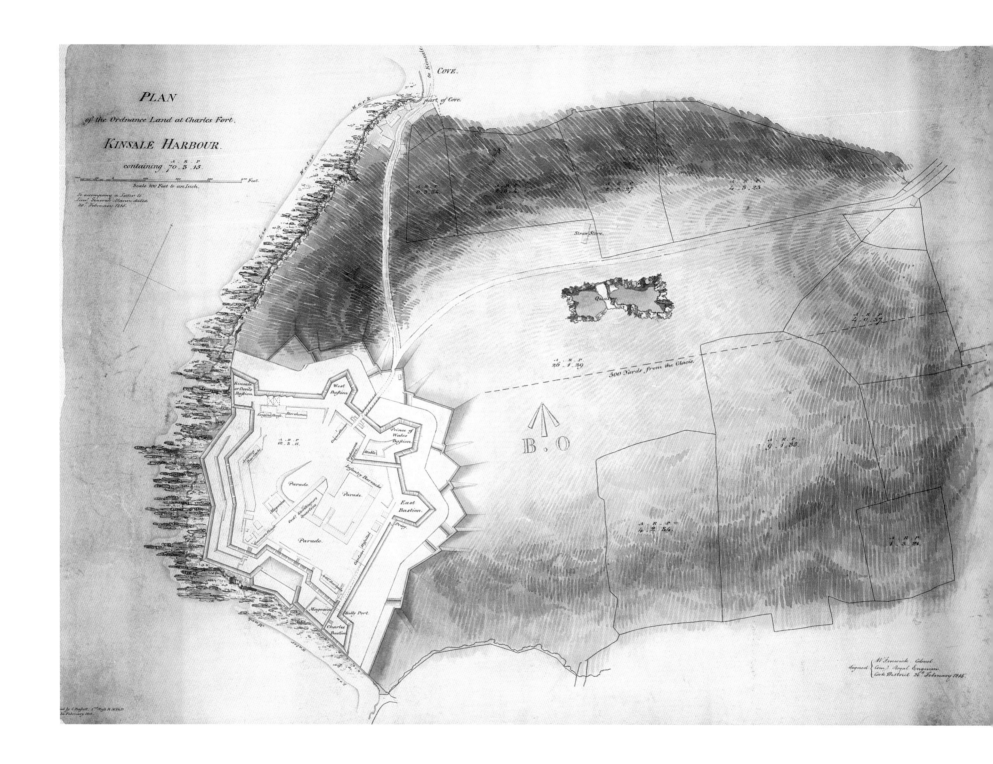

PLAN

*of the Ordnance Land at Charles Fort.*

KINSALE HARBOUR.

*containing* 70 . 3 . 13.

COVE.

*part of Cove.*

Kinsale or Devils Bastion.

West Bastion.

Prince of Wales Bastion.

East Bastion.

Charles Bastion.

Parade.

Parade.

Parade.

Infantry Barracks.

Sally Port.

300 Yards from the Glacis.

B.O

109

DUNLEARY

*Plan of part of the*

# BAY of DUBLIN

*extending from*

DUNLEARY to SANDY COVE,

*with the*

Piers

*of the*

NEW HARBOUR of DUNLEARY.

London, 10ᵗʰ May 1820.          John Rennie.

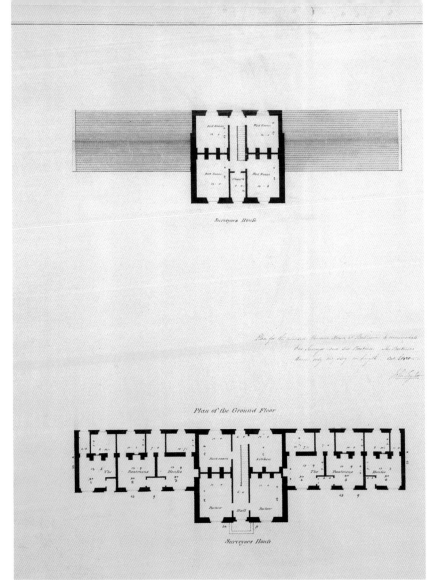

## Dunleary 1820

**Left:** Located to the south of Dublin at the extreme south of Dublin Bay, Dun Laoghaire is today an important fishing and ferry port — with connections to Holyhead — as well as a seaside resort. The still small town became known as Kingstown following a visit by King George IV in 1821, and was to gain its present name in the 1920s. The harbor, with east and west piers, was constructed between 1817 and 1821 to the designs of John Rennie (the Elder). This map shows the new harbor then under construction; it was drawn to a scale of 270 feet to one inch and is dated May 10, 1820. John Rennie (1761-1821) was a civil engineer, responsible for a number of canals in Britain; these included the Kennet & Avon and the Lancaster. His canal work was noted for the considerable style with which he embellished the structures, such as aqueducts, that he designed. His son, John (later Sir John) Rennie, was also a famous civil engineer; his work included surveying the Liverpool & Manchester Railway and London Bridge. It was after the completion of the latter, in 1831, that he was knighted.

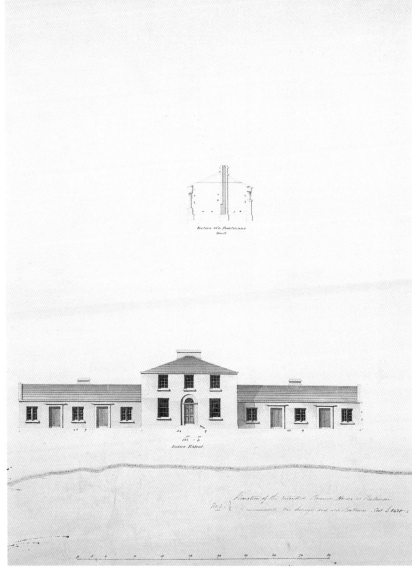

## Baltimore 1821

**Above Left and Above:** Situated in County Cork, the largest of the counties within the Province of Munster, Baltimore is, to all intents and purposes, the most southwesterly point of the Irish mainland. These four drawings, showing the plans, elevation and cross-section, illustrate houses proposed for construction at Baltimore on behalf of the Revenue. The total cost, to accommodate six boatmen and one supervisor, was £1,420. The scale of the drawings, produced by the architect John Taylor, was about 11 feet to one inch. These Revenue Houses were designed to accommodate officers whose task was to prevent smuggling.

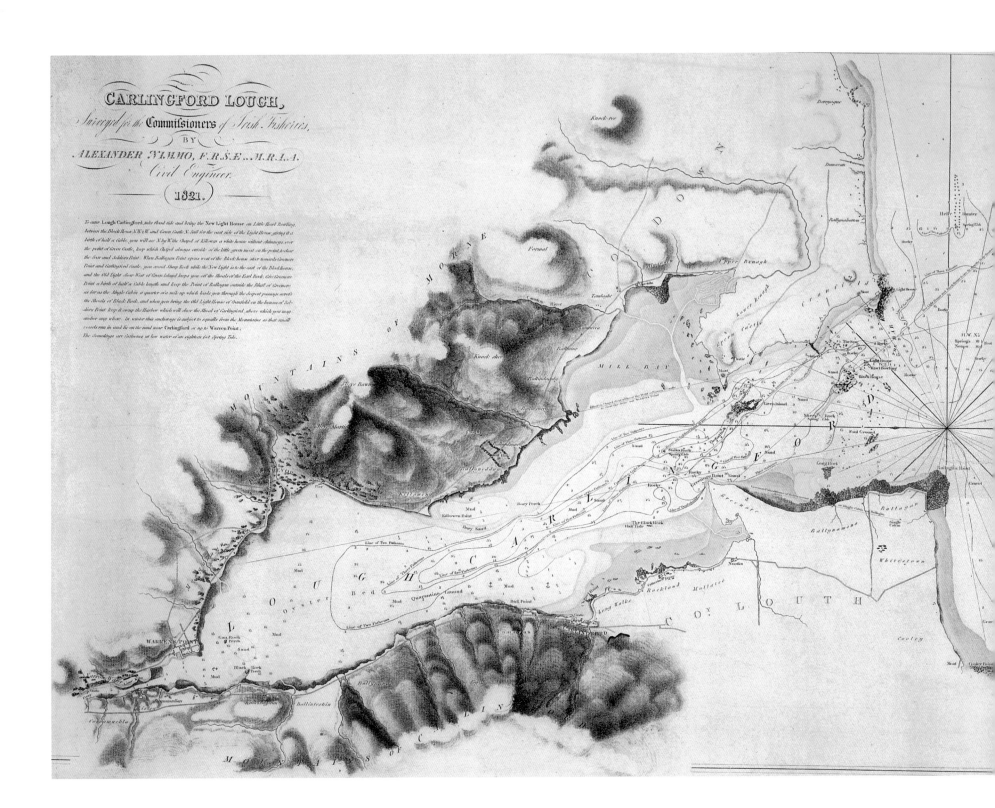

CARLINGFORD LOUGH,

*Surveyed for the* Commissioners *of Irish Fisheries,*

BY

ALEXANDER NIMMO, F.R.S.E....M.R.I.A.

*Civil Engineer.*

1821.

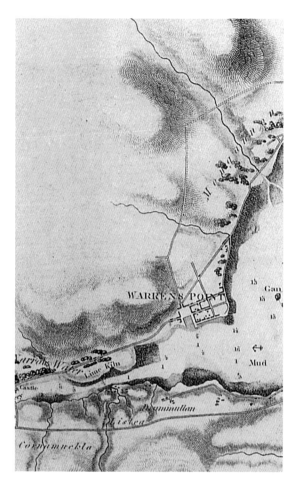

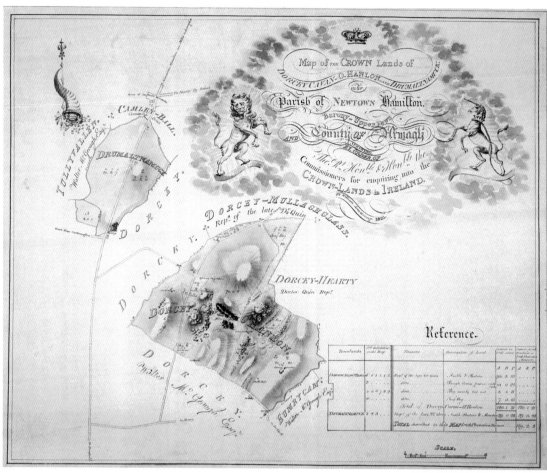

## Carlinford Lough 1821

**Left and Above (detail):** Situated at the extreme north of County Louth, the most northerly of the counties of the Province of Leinster, Carlingford Lough today forms part of the boundary between the Republic of Ireland and Northern Ireland. At the head of the Lough is Warrenpoint, while on the north (Ulster) side of the lough are Rostrevor and the Mourne Mountains. This map is one of a series produced by Alexander Nimmo for the Commissioners of Irish Fisheries. It was engraved by Wilson Lowry. Apart from the essential soundings to provide information regarding the depth of the water on the approaches to the Lough, instructions are also provided as a guide to navigation.

## Newton Hamilton 1821

**Above:** This is a map of the crown lands in the Parish of Newton Hamilton in Armagh, covering the districts of Dorcey Cavan, O'Hanlan and Drumaltnamuck. Historically, ultimate title to all land belonged to the crown and individual land ownership was based upon grants from the monarch to favored aristocrats and supporters. Gradually, however, this feudal pattern of land ownership disintegrated and land owners started to own the freehold to their own property. Much land was sold by the monarchs to replenish royal coffers at times of war, and over the centuries the royal estate diminished, although even today the crown owns significant estates throughout Great Britain. This map shows part of the royal holding of land at the time of King George IV in Armagh. It was drawn by William Armstrong and illustrates the actual holdings as well as the various tenants who occupied the land at the time. The scale is 20 chains to one inch. Also annotated are the holders of the land surrounding the royal estate. Note the crown supported by the stylized line and unicorn; these were, and still are today, symbols of the British royal family.

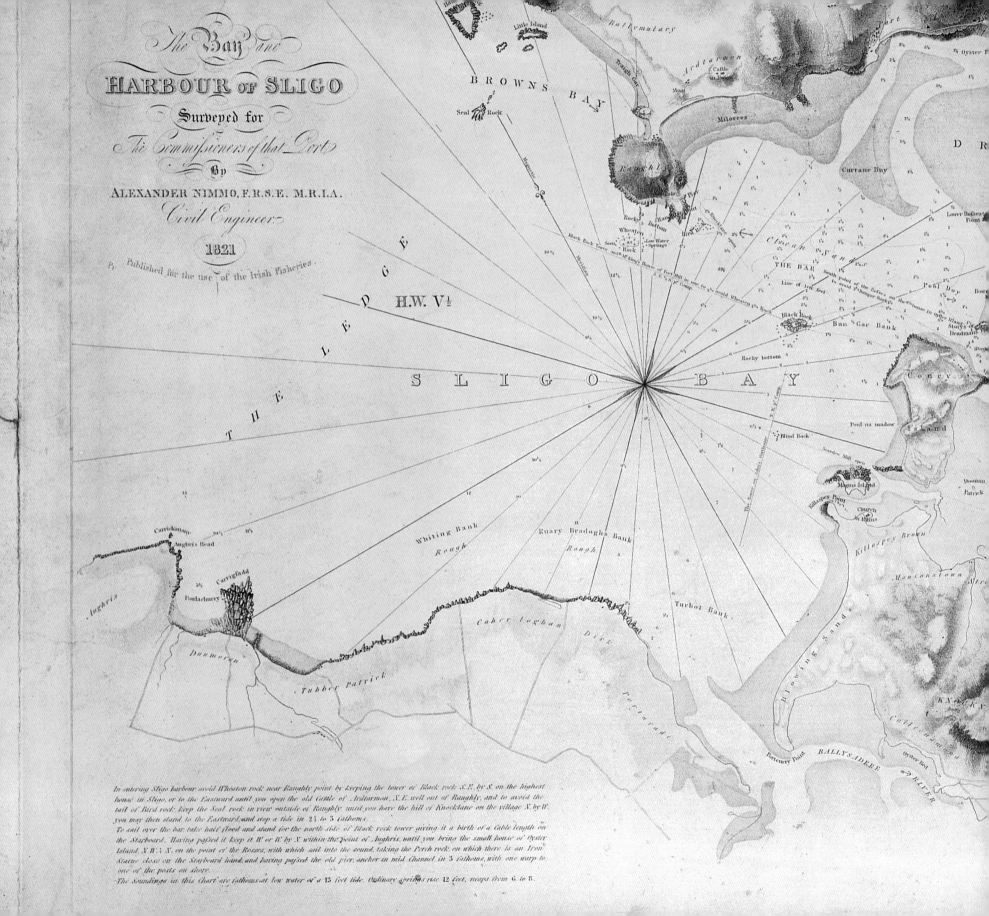

The Bay and
HARBOUR of SLIGO
Surveyed for
The Commissioners of that Port
By
ALEXANDER NIMMO, F.R.S.E. M.R.I.A.
Civil Engineer.
1821
Published for the use of the Irish Fisheries.

BROWNS BAY

SLIGO BAY

In entering Sligo harbour, avoid Wheaten rock near Raughly point by keeping the tower of Black rock S.E. by S. on the highest house in Sligo, or to the Eastward until you open the old Castle of Ardtarmon, N.E. well out of Raughly, and to avoid the tail of Bird rock, keep the Seal rock in view outside of Raughly until you have the hill of Knocklane on the village N. by W. you may then stand to the Eastward, and stop a tide in 2½ to 3 fathoms.

To sail over the bar, take half flood and stand for the north side of Black rock tower giving it a birth of a cable length on the Starboard. Having passed it keep it W. or W. by N. within the point of Aughris, until you bring the small house of Oyster Island, N.W. by N. on the point of the Rosses, with which sail into the sound, taking the Perch rock on which there is an Iron Staine close on the Starboard hand, and having passed the old pier, anchor in mid Channel in 3 fathoms, with one warp to one of the posts on shore.

The Soundings in this Chart are fathoms at low water of a 13 feet tide. Ordinary springs rise 12 feet, neaps from 6 to 8.

## Sligo 1821

**Left:** Sligo is the county town of County Sligo, one of the counties which forms the Province of Munster, and is also the principal town of northwest Ireland; the position of the town can be seen in the extreme southeast of this map of Sligo Bay. This is a map, one of a series, was compiled in 1821 by Alexander Nimmo and shows proposed improvements to Sligo Bay on behalf of the Commissioners of the Port of Sligo. It shows approaches to the harbor with soundings and also provides detailed instructions for ships entering the harbor. The map was published for the use of the Irish Fisheries and again is indicative of the importance of fishing to the coastal districts of Ireland.

## Carrickfergus 1822

**Below:** A manuscript map drawn to a scale of 25 feet to one inch and copied by M. W. Lewis, it accompanied Lieutenant-General Fryer's report of February 15, 1822. By this date Carrickfergus was in use as a military depot and arsenal, a function it continued to fulfil until 1928.

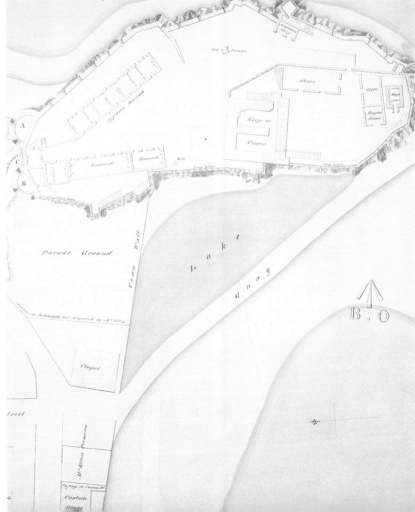

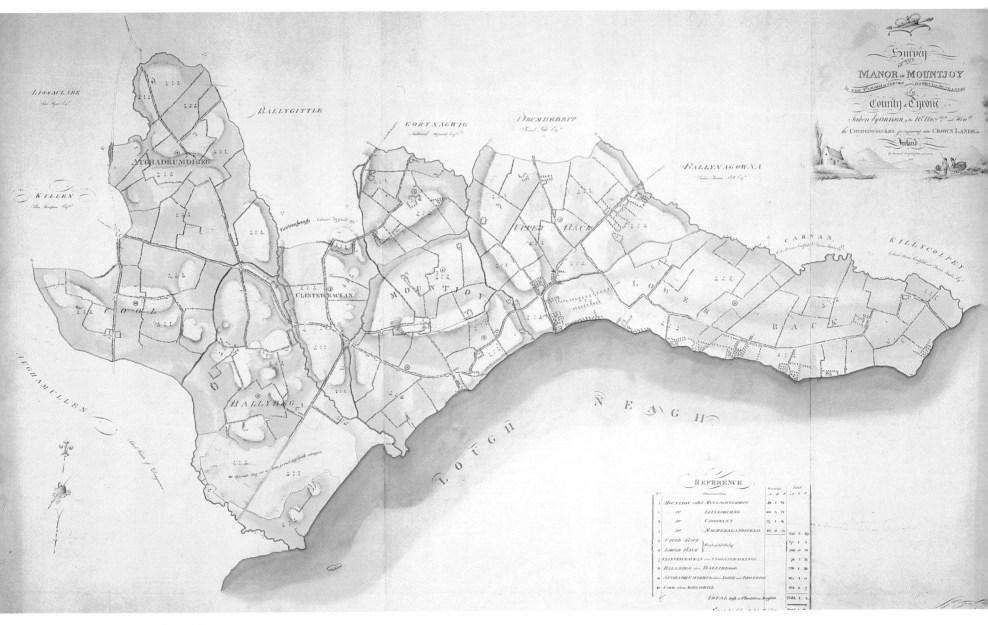

## Clonoe 1822

**Above:** The survey from which this map of Mountjoy Manor in the Barony of Dungannon, County Tyrone, was taken was by order of the Commissioners for inquiring into the Crown Lands in Ireland. The title is placed below a crown, below which is a wash drawing illustrating a lough with mountains, trees, a cottage and boatmen. The scale of the map is 16 perches to one inch. Lord Mountjoy — Charles Blount (1563-1606) succeeded as eighth Lord Mountjoy in 1594 — was the Governor of Ireland appointed in 1600 under whose control the rebellion in Ulster was finally quashed culminating the defeat of the rebels and their Spanish supporters at Kinsale. In order to maintain authority, he constructed a number of forts — including Mountjoy on the shores of Lough Neagh and Charlemont — to house garrisons.

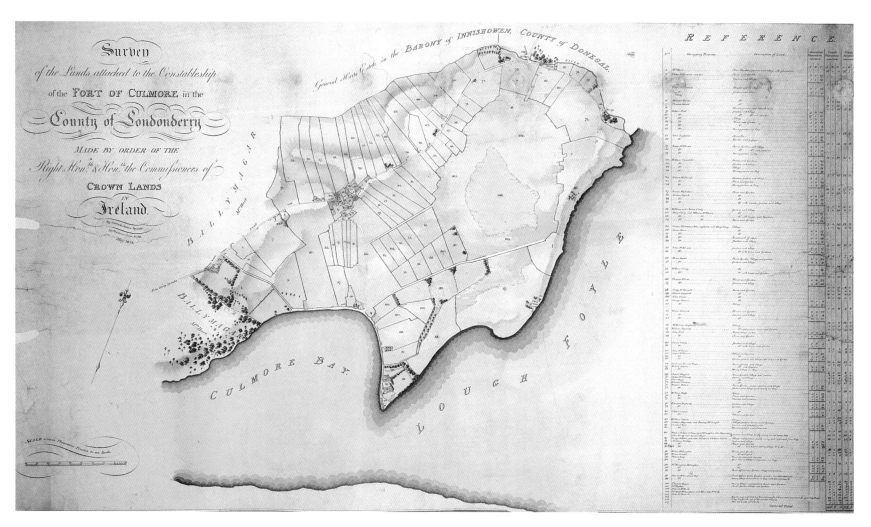

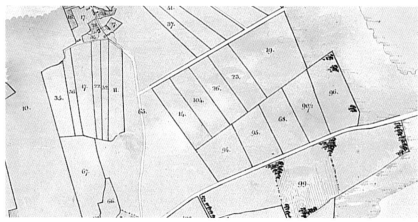

## Culmore 1825

**Above and Left (detail):** Culmore is a settlement located slightly to the northeast of Londonderry on the south side of Lough Foyle in County Londonderry. Drawn to a scale of 16 Plantation perches to one inch, this map is a survey of lands attached to the constableship of the fort at Culmore made by order of the Commissioners of Crown Lands in Ireland. It was produced by Joseph James Byrne, 39 Stephens Green North, in May 1825. The reference table gives information regarding the tenants and the nature of the occupied land.

117

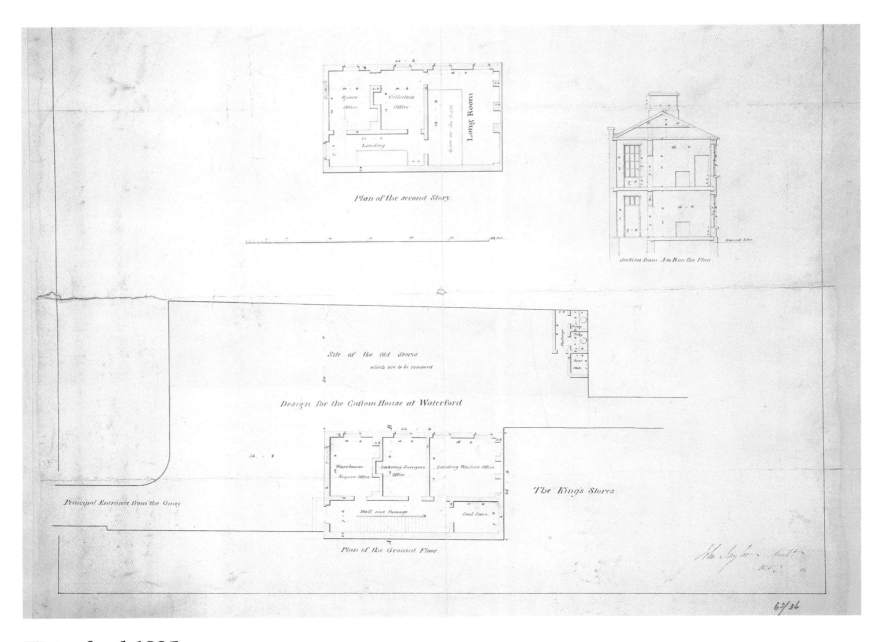

Plan of the second Story.

Section from A to B on the Plan.

Site of the Old Stores
which are to be removed

Design for the Custom House at Waterford

Long Room

The King's Stores

Principal Entrance from the Quay

Plan of the Ground Floor.

## Waterford 1825

**Above and Right:** Waterford, with a current population of some 40,000, is the county town of Waterford in the Province of Munster. It is located on the south bank of the River Suir and was founded by the Danes, as Vadrefjord, in 853 AD. Following the rise of the Anglo-Norman presence in Ireland, Waterford was to become one of the pivotal points to the Anglo-Norman hegemony in Ireland. Its motto — *Urbs intacta manet Waterfordia* ("The town of Waterford

remains intact") — was granted by King Henry VII in 1487 in response to the town's support for the new Tudor king against the claims of two pretenders to the throne. Today, Waterford is perhaps best known for its glassware — Waterford crystal. These two drawings, produced by John Taylor in the mid-1820s, show the elevation and ground plan for a proposed new Customs House in the town.

# The Elevation of the intended Custom House

## Waterford          shewing the Entrance

John Taylor

1825

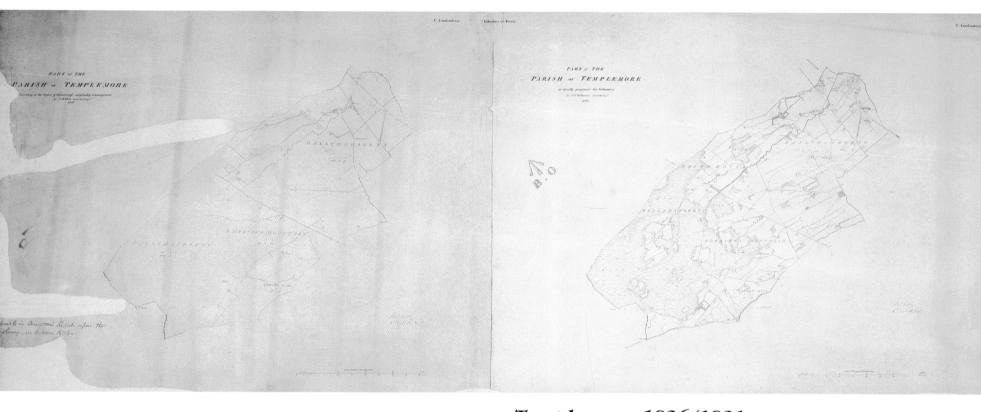

## Templemore 1826/1831

**Above Left and Above:** Here two maps of the parish of Templemore — the first being the original and the second as finally prepared for valuation — are joined together. The first was completed by Lieutenant A. D. White of the Royal Engineers in 1836 and the second by Lieutenant C. E. Wilkinson, also of the Royal Engineers, five years later. Both have been counter-signed by Lieutenant-Colonel Thomas Colby of the Royal Engineers. They are drawn to the scale of one-sixth of a mile to one inch. The Parish of Templemore is situated in the County of Tipperary, one of the six counties of the Province of Munster.

## Charlemont District 1827

**Right:** Drawn to a scale of two miles to one inch, this map shows the Ordnance and Barrack stations in County Armagh and the neighboring districts. During the first half of the 19th century the Irish economy expanded considerably, as did the population; it was only with the Great Famine of the mid-1840s that massive emigration commenced. Despite the supposed stability that increasing prosperity brought, there was still a need to ensure security. However, the period witnessed many reforms — Catholic Emancipation, parliamentary representation, education and land — things that, had it not been for the famine, could have led to a more harmonious relationship between the varying traditions in Ireland.

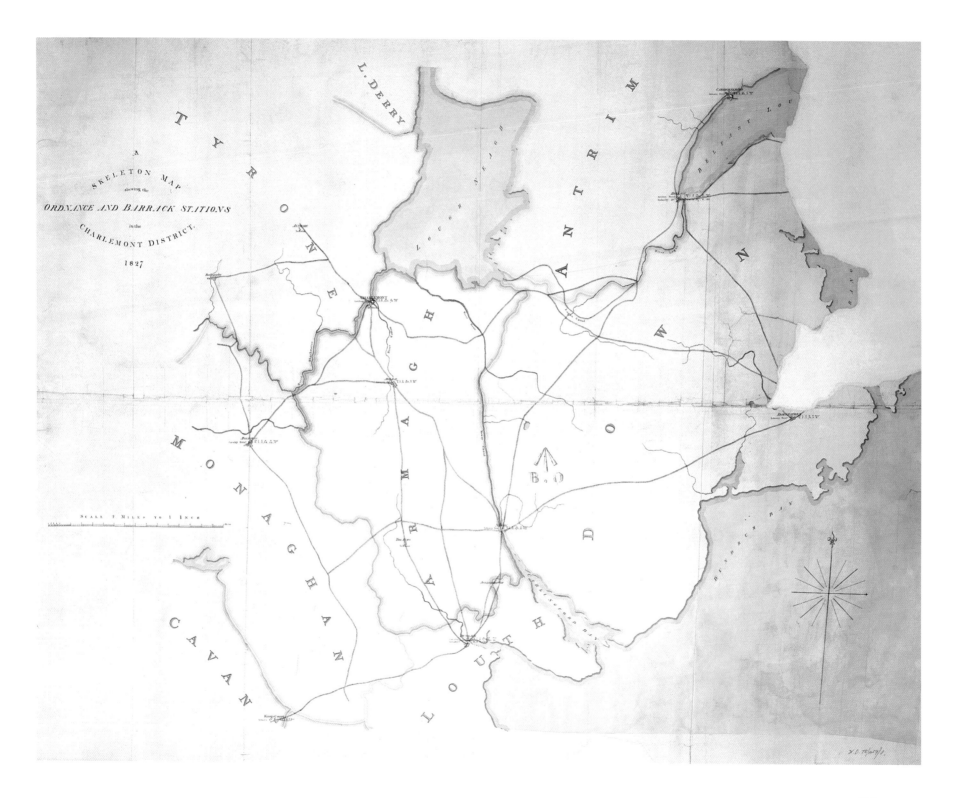

A
SKELETON MAP
shewing the
ORDNANCE AND BARRACK STATIONS
in the
CHARLEMONT DISTRICT.
1827

SCALE 7 MILES TO 1 INCH

121

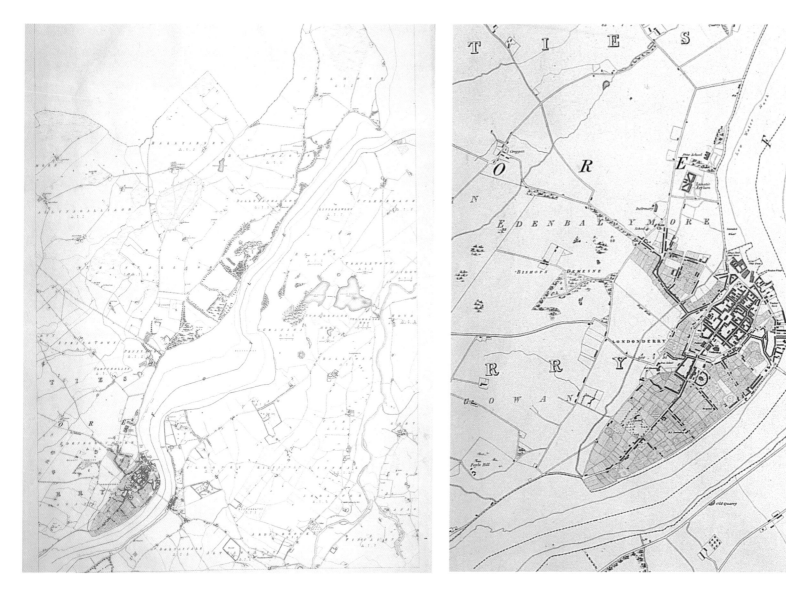

## Londonderry 1827

**Above and Above Right (detail):** This is one of a number of maps which together form the Townland Survey of County Londonderry and which were surveyed by and engraved at the Ordnance Survey Office, Phoenix Park, Dublin between 1826 and 1831. They were drawn to a scale of one-sixth of a mile to an inch. This extract shows the city of Londonderry (Derry) and its surrounding countryside. Comparison with the earlier map of the city, shown on page 81, illustrates the fact that the vast defensive works proposed in 1799 were never completed. The strategic importance of the city (with the crossing of the River Foyle) is evident, as is the relative smallness of the city at this stage.

## Dublin District 1828

**Right:** Dublin and its surrounding counties — the Pale (which effectively encompassed an area from Dundalk north of Dublin to Dun Laoghaire south of Dublin and the inland arc linking those two points) — was the center of English power in Ireland from the Middle Ages. As the administrative center of the country, it was inevitable that a sizeable military establishment would be based in the area and this map, drawn and signed by C. A. E. Graham, illustrates the Ordnance and Barrack stations in County Dublin and the surrounding areas. Drawn to a scale of two miles to one inch, it is dated February 20, 1828.

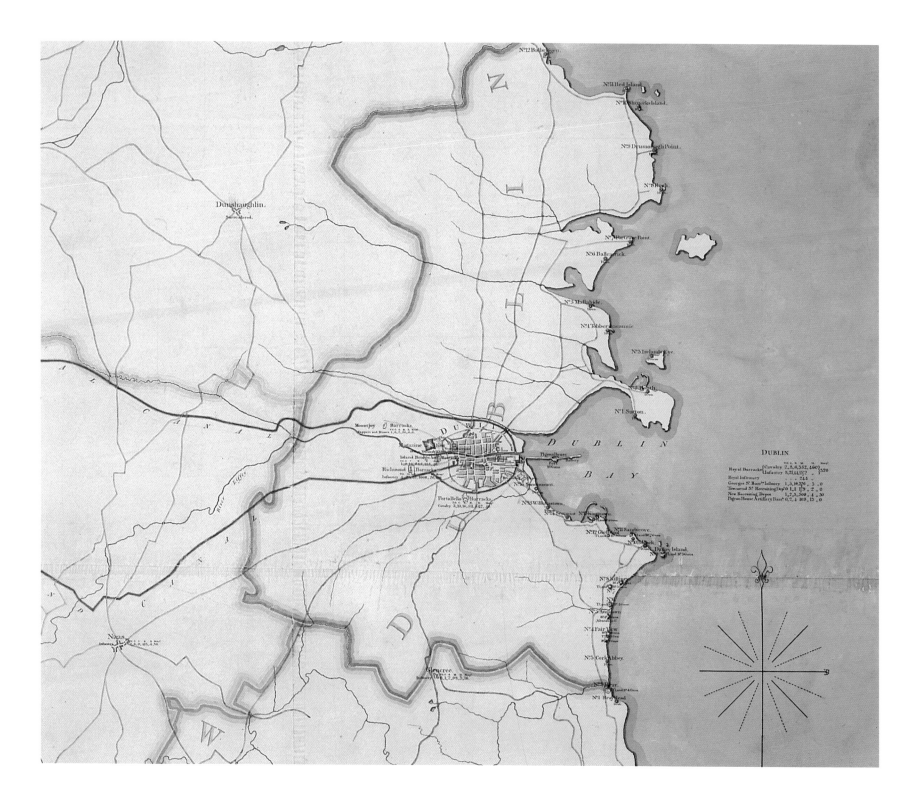

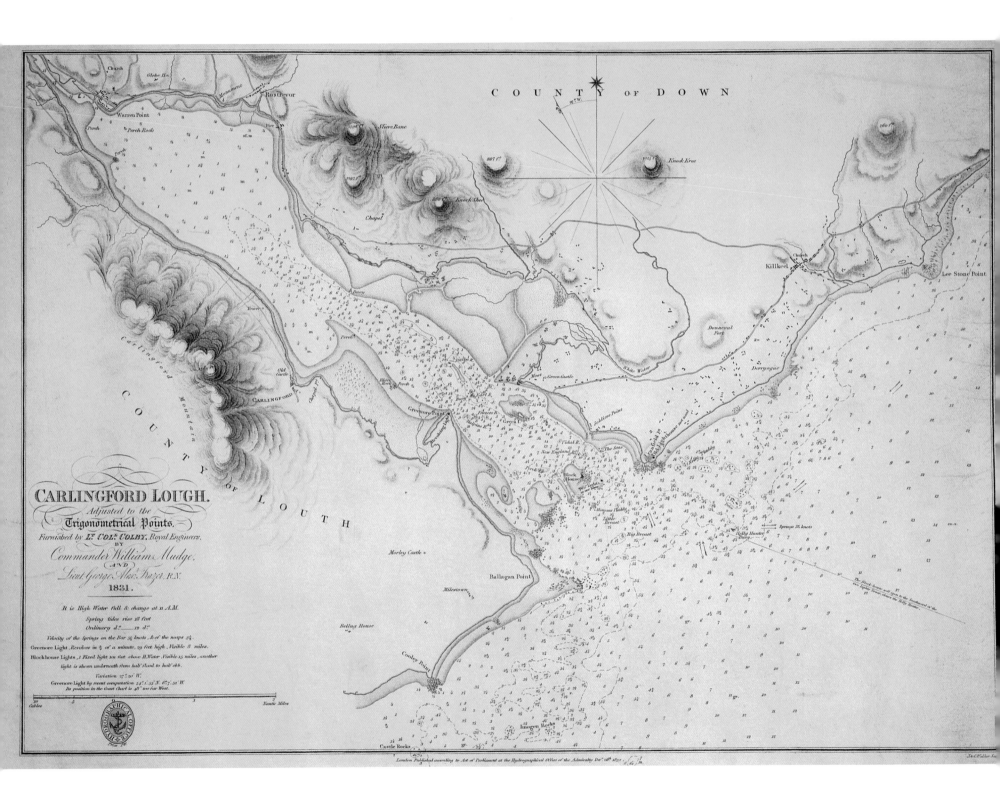

COUNTY OF DOWN

CARLINGFORD LOUGH.
Adjusted to the
Trigonometrical Points.
Furnished by Lt. Col. Colby, Royal Engineers.
BY
Commander William Mudge,
AND
Lieut. George Alex. Frazer, R.N.
1831.

It is High Water full & change at 11 A.M.
Spring tides rise 18 feet
Ordinary d⁰ 12 d⁰
Velocity of the Springs on the Bar 3½ knots, & of the neaps 2½
Greenore Light Revolves in ½ of a minute, 29 feet high, Visible 8 miles.
Blockhouse Lights 1 Fixed light 20 feet above H.Water Visible 15 miles, another
light is shewn underneath from half flood to half ebb.
Variation 27° 20' W.
Greenore Light by recent computation 54° 1' 53" N. 67° 1' 32" W.
Its position in the Great Chart is 48" too far West.

COUNTY OF LOUTH

Killkeel

Lee Stone Point

Carlingford

CARLINGFORD

124

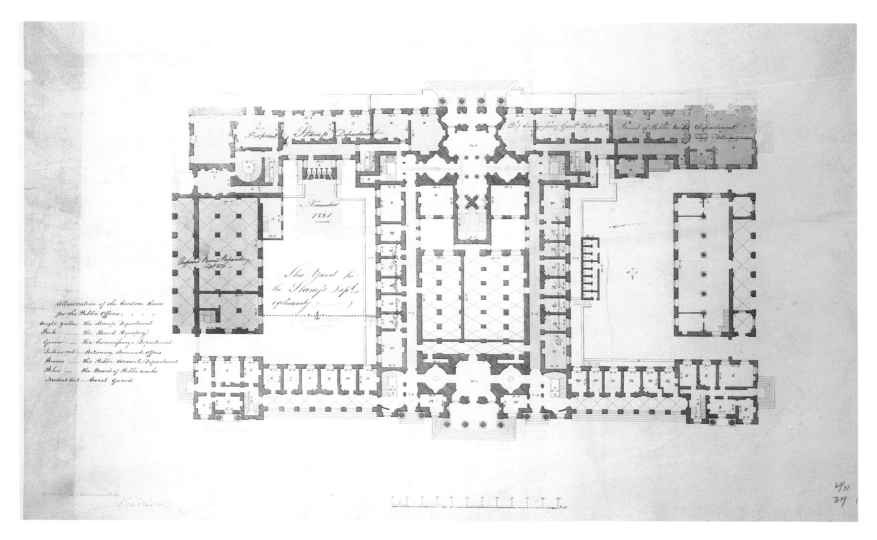

## Carlingford Lough 1831

**Left:** This is another map featuring Carlingford Lough, situated between Counties Louth and Down (see also pages 112 and 113). This map was adjusted to the trigonometrical points furnished by Lieutenant-Colonel T. F. Colby, Roal Engineers, and compiled by Commander William Mudge and Lieutenant George Alexander Fraser, both of the Royal Navy. It was engraved by J. & C. Walker and published by the Hydrographical Department of the Admiralty on December 26, 1832. The maritime nature of this map is all too evident from the precise measurements of depth and the information regarding tides.

## Dublin 1831

**Above:** Drawn to a scale of 19 feet to one inch, this is one of a series of four engraved illustrations showing the Custom House in Dublin. The original plans were drawn by Samuel Johnston. It shows the ground floor of the building and has been color-coded to illustrate which areas are occupied by specific departments: yellow for the Stamp Department; pink for the Record Depository; green for the Commissary's Department; red for the Stationary (sic) stores and offices; brown for the Public Accounts Department; blue for the Board of Public Works; and "neutral tint" for the Coast Guard. The Custom House, designed by James Gandon (1743–1823), is situated on the north bank of the River Liffey on, appropriately, Custom House Quay. An Englishman of French Huguenot (ie Protestant) ancestry, Gandon was the architect behind a number of many buildings in Dublin. The building was severely damaged during the Civil War in 1921 and was subsequently restored.

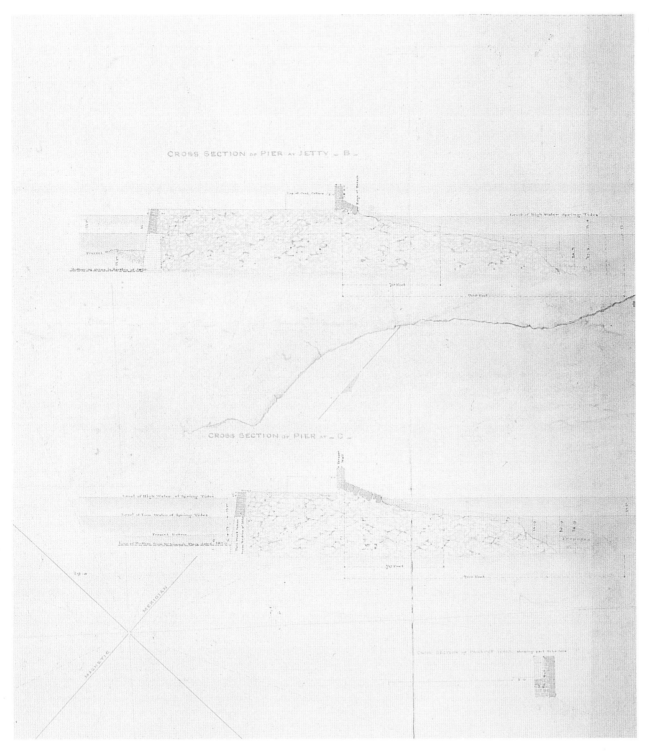

CROSS SECTION of PIER at JETTY _ B _

CROSS SECTION of PIER at _ C _

## Dunmore East 1832

**Left and Far Left:** This is a survey of the pier and harbor at Dunmore East, in County Waterford, drawn by George Halpin. Apart from showing a plan of the actual pier and harbor drawn at 66 feet 8 inches to one inch, the illustration also includes cross-sections of the pier drawn at 30 feet to one inch. Dunmore East is located to the south of Waterford itself on the western side of the approaches to Waterford Harbor. Today, Dunmore East is a seaside resort possessing a small harbor with beach. Good facilities for diving are among other attractions it offers.

## Southwest Ireland 1837

**Right:** Although the first half of the 19th century was characterized by the growing belief in *laissez faire* in trade and industry, the British government was not averse to undertaking a more positive role in commercial and social developments. Without a doubt, the creation of the railways represented a major contribution to the industrialization of mainland Britain and, by the mid-1830s, it was clear that railways were going to replace water as the major means of transportation. For Ireland, the railways also had a potentially strategic importance, giving the authorities an opportunity to move men and munitions quickly. This map, and the next pair, are samples of the maps produced by the Irish Railway Commissioners in 1837 when determining the development of railways throughout the island. This first map shows the lines proposed to serve the district to the south and west of Dublin. It was prepared by the civil engineer Charles Vignoles. Charles Blacker Vignoles (1793–1875) was an Irishman, born in County Wexford, who served with the British army. For a period, while still nominally an officer (he went on half pay in 1816), he worked in the USA before returning to the British Isles in 1825. He was involved with the Liverpool & Manchester Railway, before acting as engineer for the Dublin & Kingstown Railway — the first railway in Ireland, which opened on December 17, 1834. Apart from his work with the Irish Railway Commissioners, he also advised on the building of railways in Europe and was the first professor of civil engineering at University College, London.

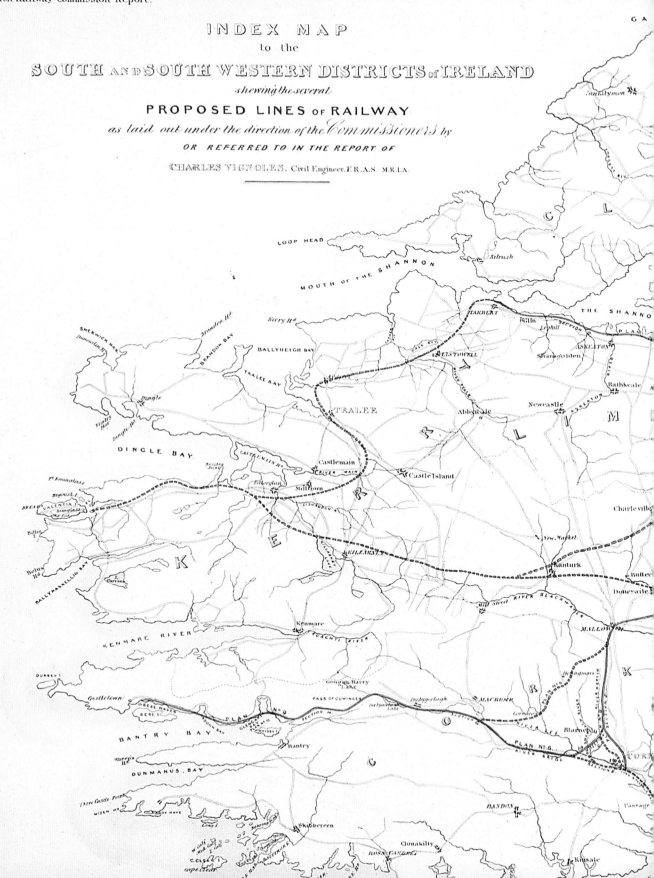

INDEX MAP to the SOUTH AND SOUTH WESTERN DISTRICTS OF IRELAND shewing the several PROPOSED LINES OF RAILWAY as laid out under the direction of the Commissioners by OR REFERRED TO IN THE REPORT OF CHARLES VIGNOLES, Civil Engineer, F.R.A.S M.R.I.A.

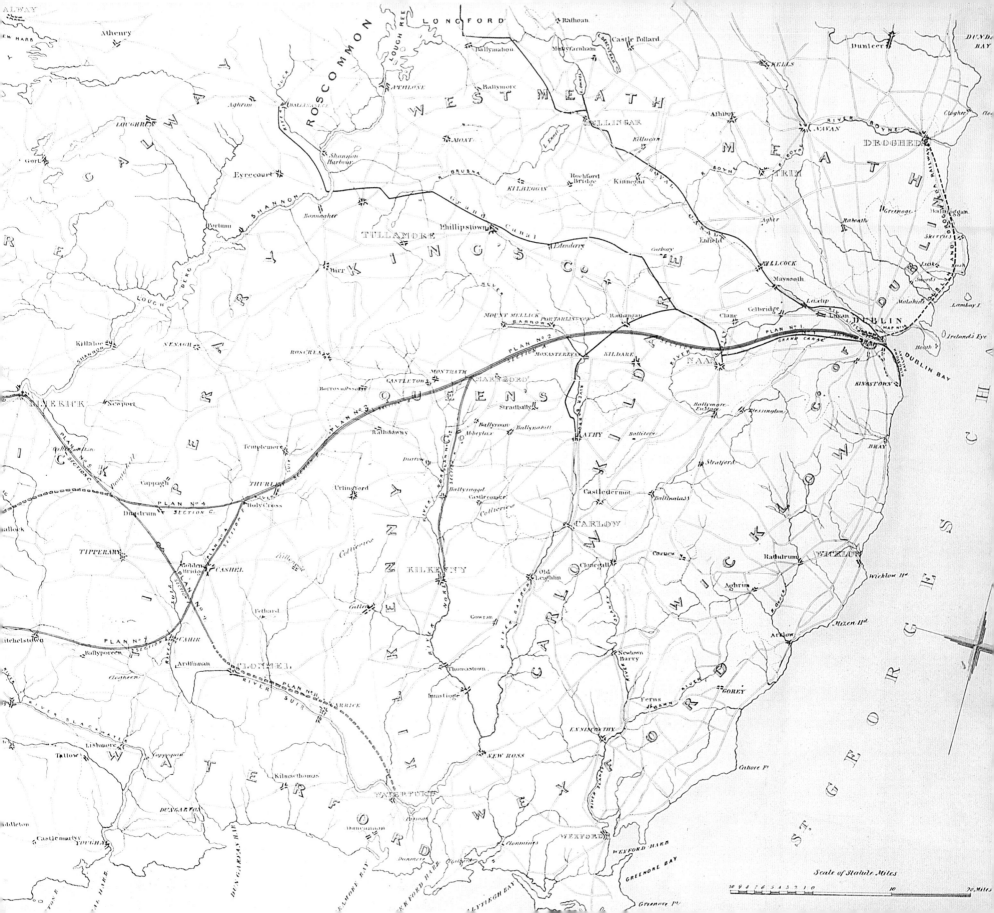

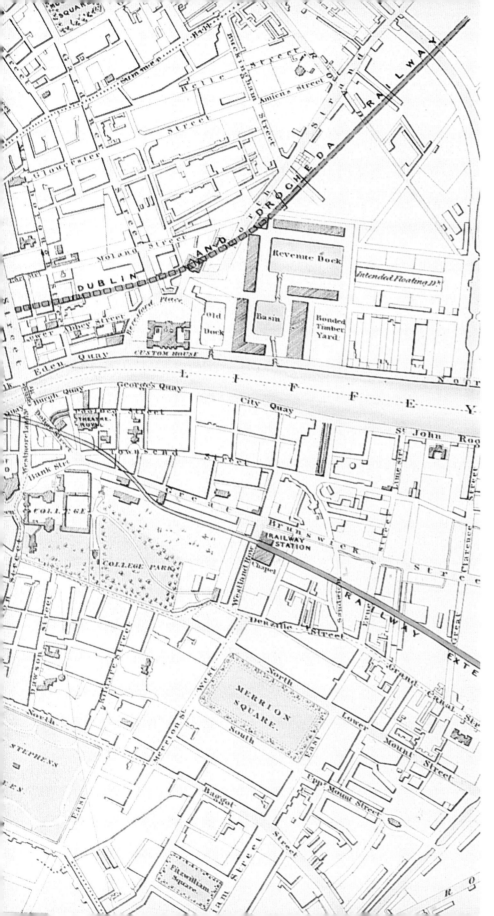

## Dublin 1837

**Left:** This is a second map from the survey undertaking by the Irish Railway Commissioners, presented to parliament in 1837. It shows the proposed construction of railways in Dublin. By the date of this map, the first railway in Ireland — the Dublin & Kingstown Railway — had opened; this is the line shown in blue heading southeastward. The railway station mentioned is Westland Row. The D&KR was originally built to the British standard gauge of 4 feet 8.5 inches, but was converted to the Irish standard gauge of 5 feet 3 inches in 1855. North of the River Liffey is the Dublin & Drogheda Railway; this was opened from a temporary station to Drogheda on May 26, 1844; the temporary station was replaced by Amiens Street (Connolly) station on November 29, 1844. The D&DR and D&KR were eventually to be connected with a viaduct over the Liffey. To the west of the center is the future line from Kingsbridge (renamed Heuston in 1966) towards Cork; the first section of this line was opened by the Great South Western Railway on August 4, 1846.

## Dublin 1837

**Below:** This is a further extract from the maps produced by the Irish Railway Commission and shows the proposals for constructing a connecting line between the existing Dublin & Kingstown Railway and those proposed to serve southwest Ireland from a new station at Barrack Street. The proposal, again planned by the engineer Charles Vignoles, was for a viaduct running parallel to the River Liffey that would incorporate (like the Embankment in London) improvements to the actual river bank. Reflecting the prominent position that this viaduct would occupy, Vignoles has chosen the highly classical architectural style much in vogue in the 1830s. In the event, this structure was never completed.

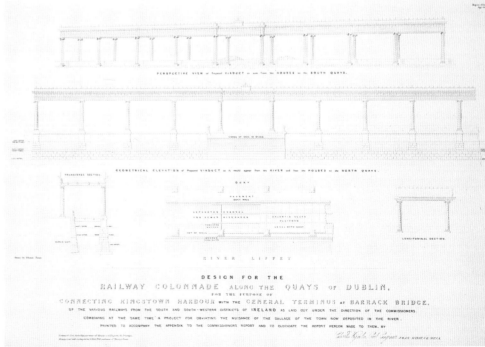

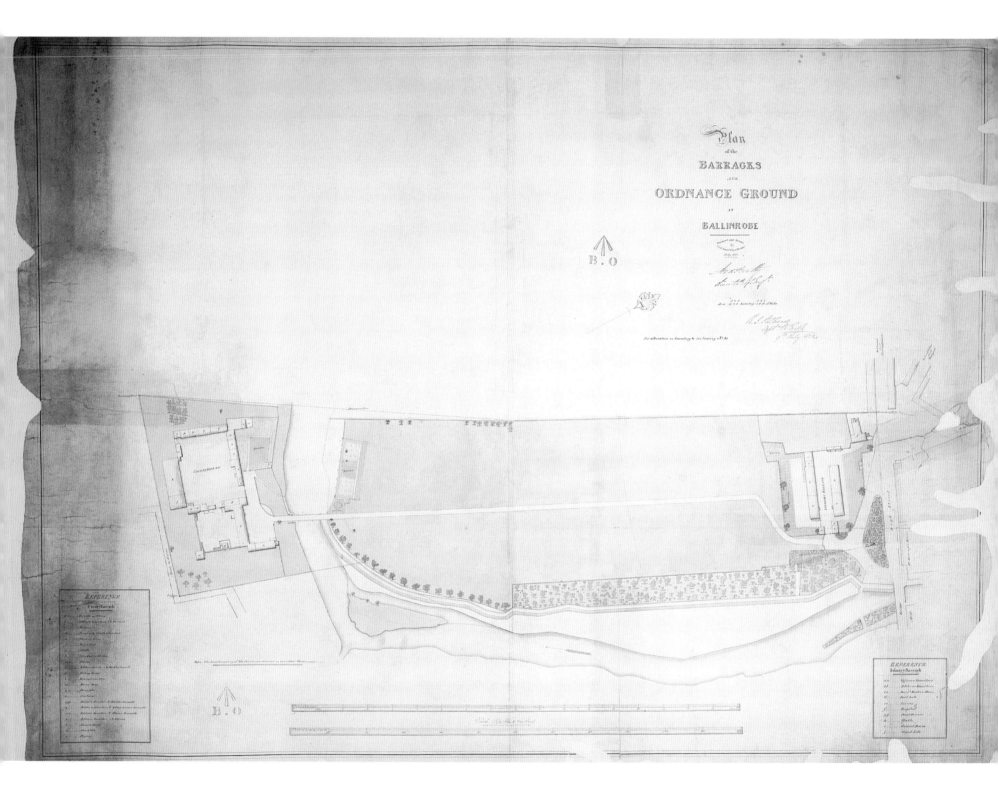

Plan
of the
BARRACKS
AND
ORDNANCE GROUND
AT
BALLINROBE

B.O

B.O

132

## Ballinrobe 1838

**Far left:** Ballinrobe, County Mayo, is located on the River Robe — hence its Gaelic name. This is a plan of the Barracks and Ordnance ground at Ballinrobe. Drawn to a scale of 50 feet to one inch, it was surveyed and drawn by Cornelius Devine, Civil Assistant, in July 1838. It has been countersigned by Lieutenant A. Beatty and Captain R. J. Stotherd, both of the Royal Engineers, and dated July 9, 1842.

## Lower Malone 1840

**Left:** Lower Malone is situated in County Antrim and this map, drawn by Robert Pattison in 1840, shows the property held in the district by Miss Gregg and the relationship of her property with that held by other landowners. A table of references provides information on the holdings of individual tenant farmers. The map is drawn to the scale of eight Irish perches to one inch. The question of landownership — particularly that of absentee landowners — was to dominate much of the period of British rule in Ireland, leading to considerable friction and violence. Later in the 19th century, "boycott" was to emerge as a word reflecting rent strikes and the ostracization of landlords from community activity. It was derived from one of the most notable victims of this activity, Captain Charles Cunningham Boycott (1832-97), who, after a career in the army, became agent in County Mayo for Lord Erne. Of all the districts of Ireland, those that suffered least from the agrarian outrages of the late 19th century were those — Londonderry, Antrim and Down — which had a Protestant majority. It was no coincidence that the future six counties of Northern Ireland were those where land disputes were less troublesome.

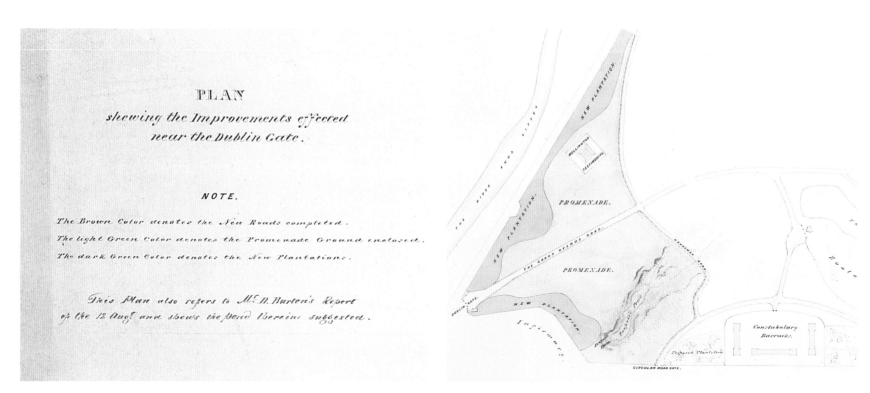

PLAN

shewing the Improvements effected
near the Dublin Gate.

NOTE.

The Brown Color denotes the New Roads completed.
The light Green Color denotes the Promenade Ground enclosed.
The dark Green Color denotes the New Plantations.

This Plan also refers to Mr. D. Burton's Report
of the 12 Aug. and shews the pond therein suggested.

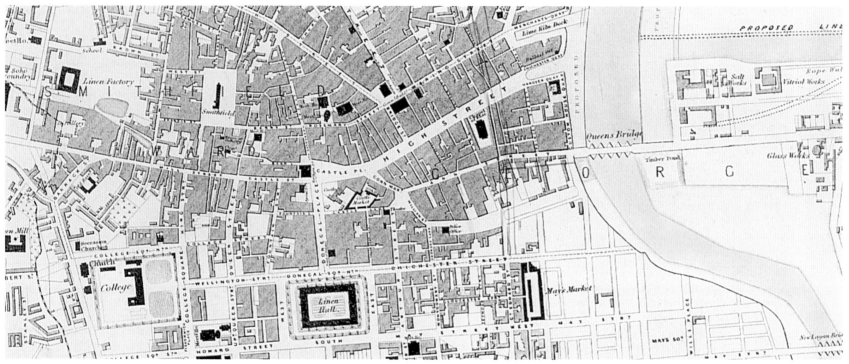

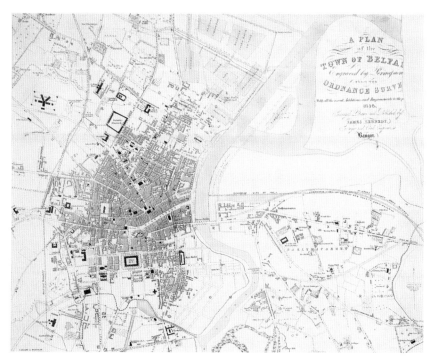

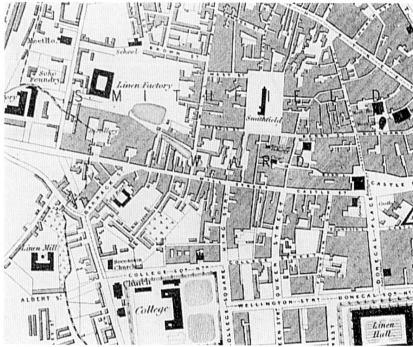

# Dublin 1843–44

**Opposite Page, Above Left and Right:** Of all the open spaces in Dublin, none is more famous than Phoenix Park, which is located to the west of the city on the north side of the River Liffey. The park, which covers almost 2,000 acres, was established by Lord Chesterfield, the then Viceroy, in the 1740s. It owes its name to the Irish name of a nearby spring — "Fionn Uisage" (which can be translated as clear water) — and not to the column surmounted by a phoenix — the legendary bird said to emerge reborn from its own ashes — erected by Lord Chesterfield in 1747. This map, one of a series delineating Phoenix Park in the early 1840s, drawn by Decimus Burton to indicate proposed improvements, shows the location of the zoological gardens and the column erected as a monument to Lord Wellington, victor at the Battle of Waterloo in 1815 and later Prime Minster of the United Kingdom. Decimus Burton was one of the leading architects and garden designers of the period. Phoenix Park, later in the 19th century, was to become notorious in the annals of Irish history. On May 6, 1882, Thomas Burke, the permanent under-secretary for Ireland, and Lord Frederick Cavendish, the newly appointed Chief Secretary, were hacked to death by assassins — called the "Invincibles" — using surgical knives. Nine murderers were later brought to trial, of whom five were hung for their part in the "Phoenix Park Murders." At the time of these murders, there was co-operation in parliament between William Gladstone, the Prime Minister, and Charles Stewart Parnell, leader of the Irish Party. However, despite Parnell's condemnation of the murders, Gladstone brought in a draconian Prevention of Crimes Act. The opportunity for a peaceful move towards Home Rule was lost.

# Belfast 1846

**Above Left and (details) Below Left and Above:** Although relatively unimportant until the Industrial Revolution, Belfast was to become the economic heart of industrial Ireland in the decades after the Act of Union. This map, based upon those drawn by the Ordnance Survey and revised, drawn, and published by James Kennedy (a surveyor and civil engineer of Bangor), illustrates the growth of Belfast by the mid-19th century. The arrival of industry is evinced by references to various textile factories and by the massive growth of the proposed dock area. The map, however, predates the establishment in 1859 of the famous Harland & Wolff shipyard, where the ill-fated *Titanic* was built just prior to World War I, as well as the construction of many of the most important public buildings (such as the Custom House, illustrated on pages 138–139). Although Belfast's prominence only really arrived with the Industrial Revolution, the town had gained its first charter from King James I in 1613 and a castle had existed to control the river crossing from the early middle ages.

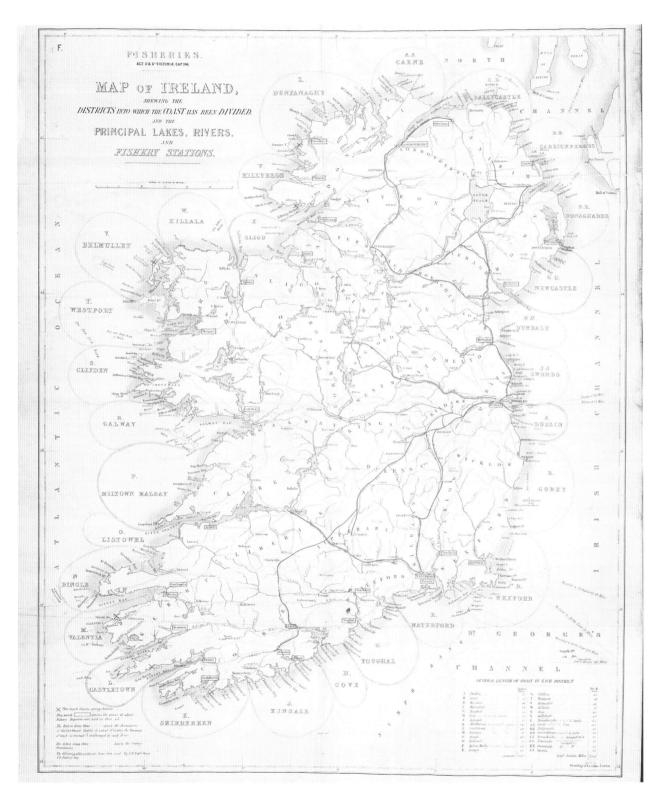

# Ireland c1846

**Left and Far Left (detail):** Drawn to a scale of 12.5 miles to one inch, this map shows the whole island of Ireland in the mid-19th century. Although of primary interest in that it shows the division of the coastal areas into fishery stations — fishing was and is an important industry for the country — it is also of interest in that it shows the extent of railway development by this stage, as well as the network of roads which also existed.

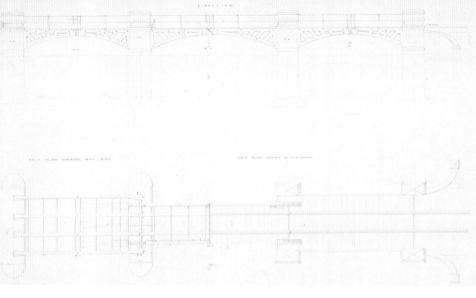

## *Newry, Warren Point & Rostrevor Railway 1846*

**Above:** By the 1840s the spread of railways through the British Isles was rapid; the decade was to witness the so-called "railway mania" when thousands of miles of railway lines were proposed and built, many of which were never to be economically successful. This map portrays one of the bridges proposed to link various settlements along the north coast of Carlingford Lough in County Down. Drawn to a scale of five feet to one inch, the drawings show the elevation and half plan of an iron bridge. Note that the plans have been signed and approved both by the Admiralty and by the Department of Woods and Forests. The railway line from Newry to Warrenpoint was opened for freight traffic on May 28, 1849, and to passenger services on the following June 16. This line was built to the standard Irish gauge of 5 feet 3 inches. The route later formed part of the Great Northern Railway (Ireland) and, following the collapse of that company, passed to the Ulster Transport Authority. It closed on January 4, 1965. Although the original railway had the name 'Rostrevor' in its title, it was not until August 1877 that the three-mile line from Warrenpoint to Rostrevor was opened. This line was built by the Warrenpoint & Rostrevor Tramways Co to the narrow gauge of 2 feet 10 inches. The line closed completely in February 1915.

## *Belfast c.1847*

**Right:** By the mid-19th century, with the Industrial Revolution, the city of Belfast began to experience rapid growth and with this came the provision of important public buildings. Among those built during the period was the Custom House, situated close to the River Lagan to the southeast of St Anne's Cathedral. The building was constructed between 1854 and 1857 in a strong classical style, its gable being surmounted by statues of Britannia, Neptune and Mercury. This drawing, one of a series, shows the "rere [sic] elevation" of the proposed building drawn to a scale of 10 feet to one inch and, dated April 28, 1847, is endorsed by Charles (later Sir Charles) Landon.

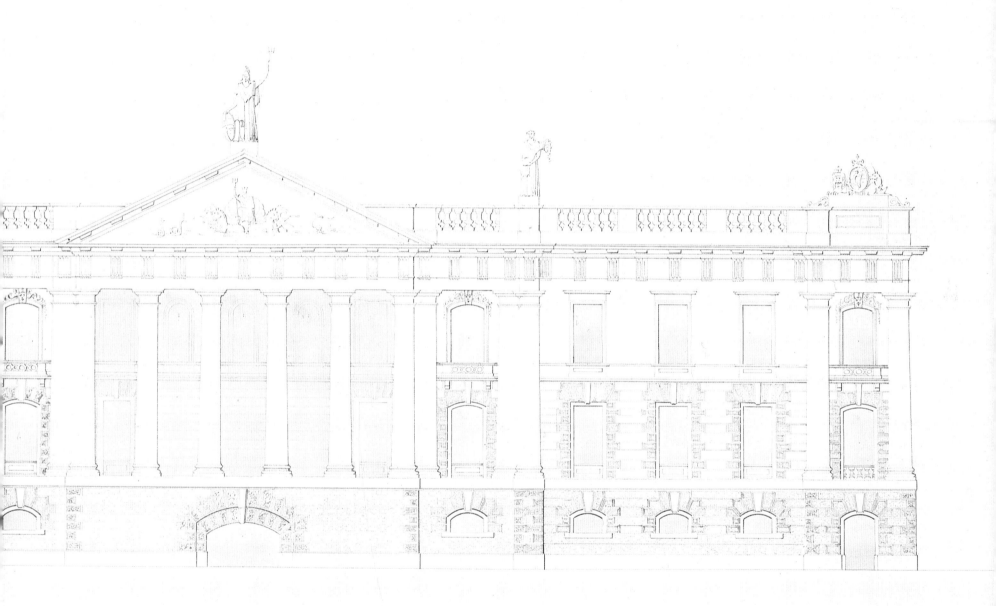

RERE - ELEVATION

SCALE TEN FEET TO AN INCH.

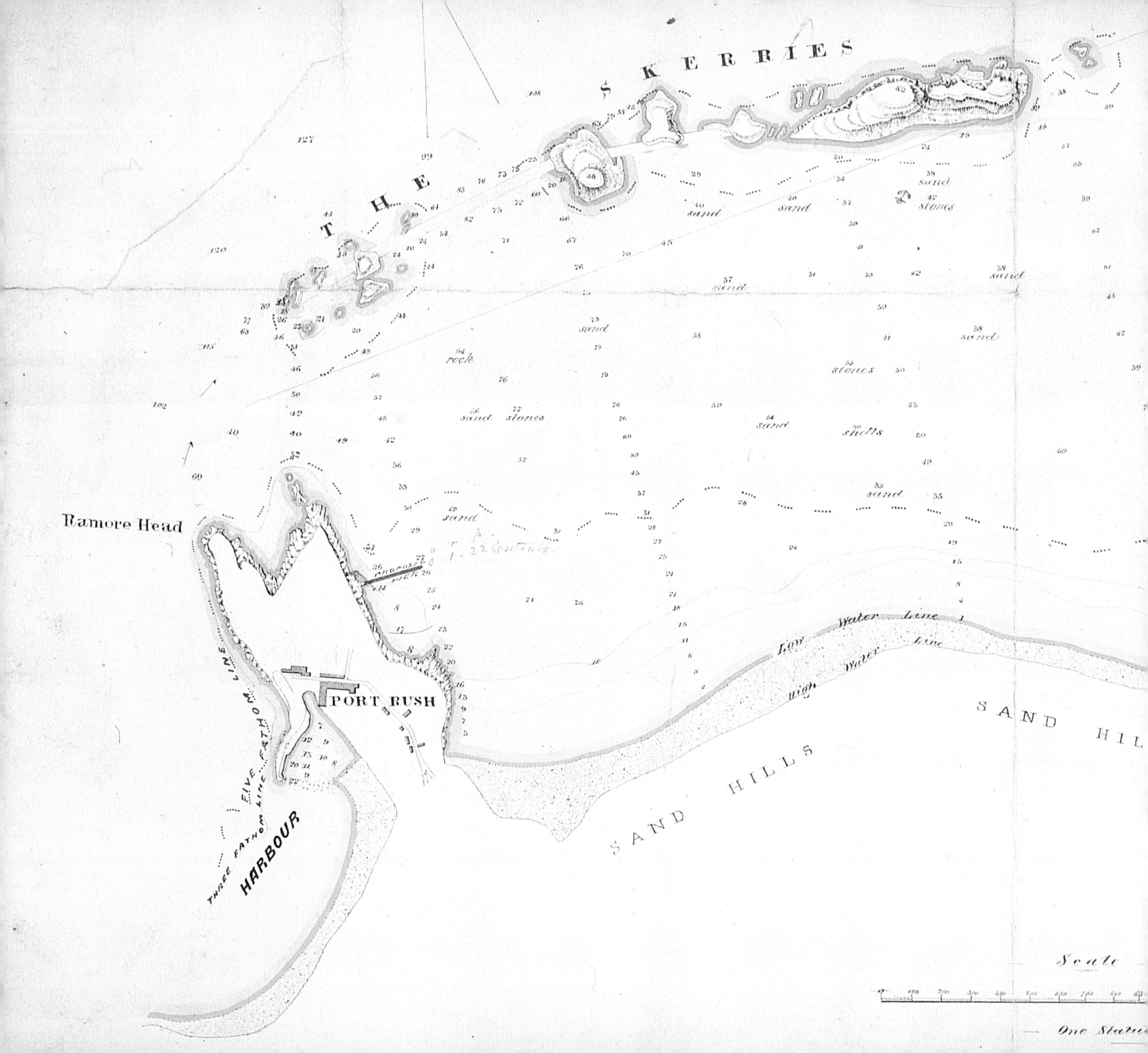

THE SKERRIES

Ramore Head

PORT RUSH

HARBOUR

FIVE FATHOM LINE

THREE FATHOM LINE

Low Water Line

High Water Line

SAND HILLS

SAND HILLS

SAND HILL

sand

sand

sand

stones

sand

shells

sand

stones

sand stones

rock

sand

Scale

0    100    200    300    400    500    600    700    800

One Statute

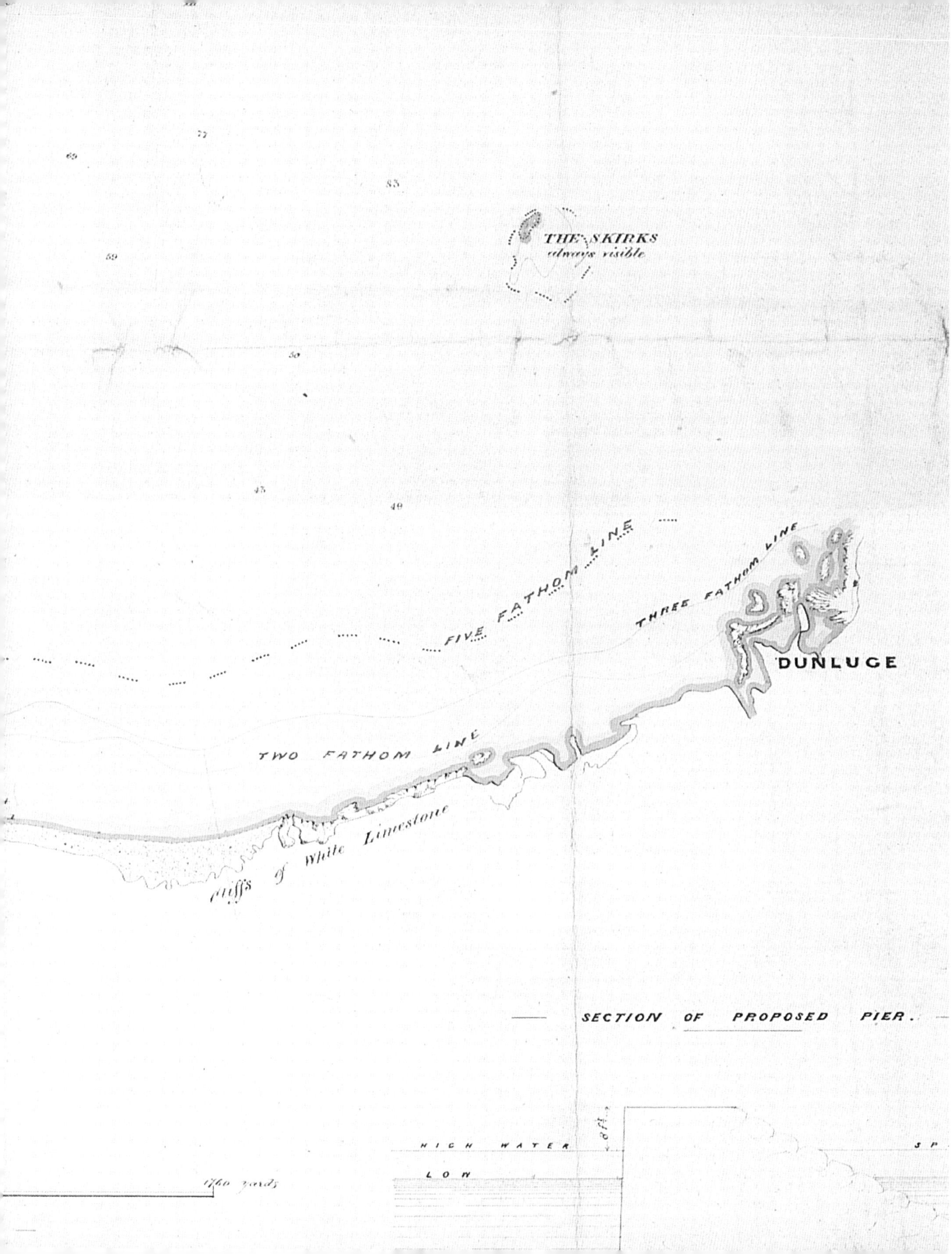

THE SKIRKS
always visible
FIVE FATHOM LINE
THREE FATHOM LINE
TWO FATHOM LINE
DUNLUGE
Cliffs of White Limestone
SECTION OF PROPOSED PIER.
HIGH WATER
LOW
1760 yards


Duplicate Drawing. To be transmitted to Mr William Dargan.

The Lords Commissioners of the Admiralty hereby assent (in so far as their Lordships' jurisdiction is concerned, and without prejudice to the Estate and Interest of Her Majesty, or other the Owner or Owners thereof in the soil of the tidal lands on which the Works are to be constructed) to the application of Mr William Dargan, for permission to construct a Pier on the East side of Ramore Head, near Portrush, as shown by the Plan and Section on this Drawing, subject to the condition, that the Work be completed within seven years from this date, and to be maintained to the satisfaction of the Admiralty.

Admiralty,
6th August, 1859

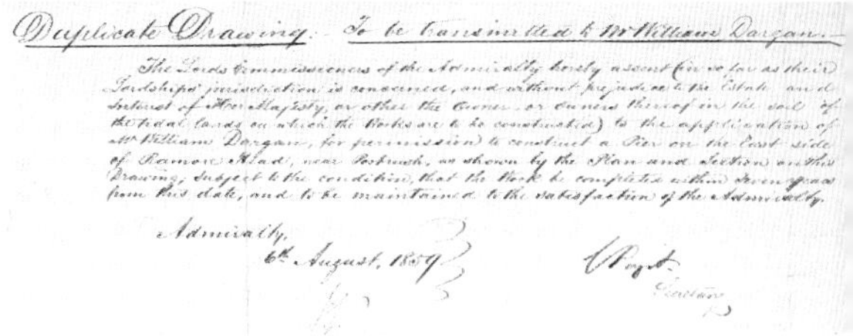

## *Portrush c.1859*

**Left and Above (detail):** This is a colored manuscript map, scaled at 300 yards to one inch, produced by John Hawkshaw on July 18, 1859 to show a proposed pier at Portrush in County Antrim. There is a section of the pier drawn at the enlarged scale of 20 feet to one inch. In addition to the features on land, the map also shows the soundings on the approaches to the planned pier. Note the assent of the Admiralty to the construction of the pier is written at the top of the plan (see detail). Many coastal and estuarial developments throughout the British Isles were dependent upon the permission of the Admiralty, which was concerned to ensure the continued access of Royal Navy ships to ports.

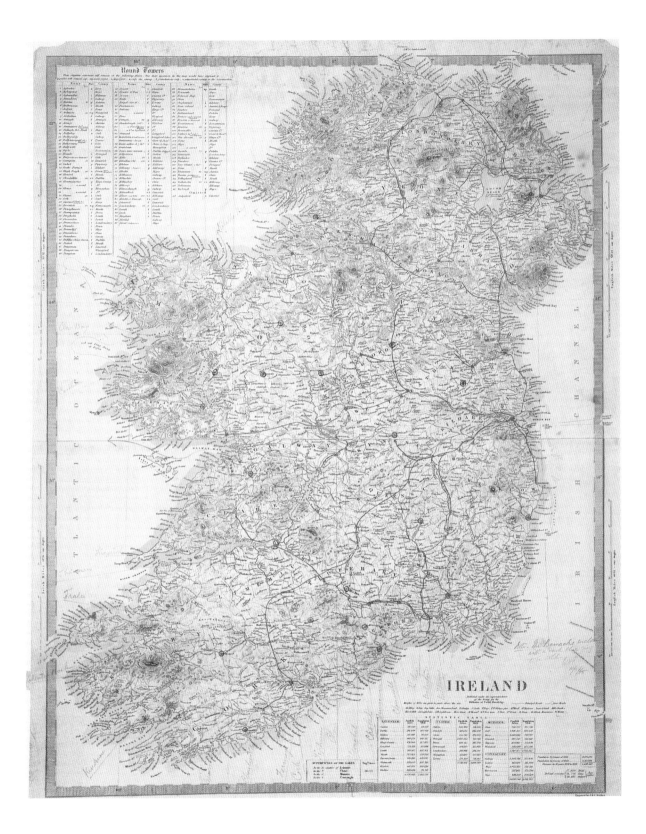

# Ireland c.1865

**Left and Far Left (detail):** This overview of the whole island of Ireland was published on behalf of the Society for the Diffusion of Useful Knowledge by Edward Stanford. Although its exact date is uncertain — possibly 1858 — the copy illustrated here has manuscript additions, which can be dated to 1865. It shows the position of army barracks and there are also reference tables to the location of round towers, population and acreage. The scale of the map, engraved by J. and C. Walker, is 12 miles to one inch. It dates to the period after the Great Famine, when the Irish population was in decline as a result of the deaths, and emigration both to the British mainland and to North America. The map also includes tabular information on the size of districts and the population, as well as indicating the routes of the various railways that had by then been completed. The highlighting of the army barracks emphasizes that, even at a time of relative peace, security was a major concern. The compilers were no doubt unaware that 1865 was the year Fenianism, one of the more violent of Irish revolutiary movements, first began to influence matters in Ireland.

# INDEX

Antrim c.1580 .................................... 34
Augher c.1610 .................................... 66
Ballincollig 1810 ................................. 96
Ballincollig 1811 ................................ 103
Ballinrobe 1838 ................................. 133
Baltimore 1821 .................................. 111
Banagher c.1600 .................................. 48
Banagher 1810 ................................... 99
Bantry Bay c1558 ................................ 22
Belfast Lough 1569 ............................... 24
Belfast 1846 .................................... 135
Belfast 1847 .................................... 138
Blackwater Fort 1587 ............................. 42
Boyne 1690 ...................................... 69
Carlingford Lough 1821 .......................... 113
Carlingford Lough 1831 .......................... 125
Carrickfergus c.1600 .............................. 48
Carrickfergus 1811 .............................. 104
Carrickfergus 1822 .............................. 115
Castlemaine 1572 ................................. 29
Cavan 1591 ...................................... 45
Charlemont c.1610 ................................ 66
Charlemont 1811 ................................ 105
Charlemount 1815 ............................... 108
Charlemont District 1827 ........................ 120
Clanawley c.1609 ................................. 53
Clankee c.1609 ................................... 53
Clankelly c.1609 ................................. 54
Clonoe 1822 .................................... 116
Cork c.1770 ..................................... 75
Cork 1781 ....................................... 76
Cork 1800/1802 .................................. 83
Cork 1803 ....................................... 84
Cork 1809 ....................................... 96
Cork 1812 ...................................... 106
Cork and Kerry 1587 .............................. 37
Corkbeg Fort c.157 .............................. 127
County Down c.1570 .............................. 24
County Down c.1580 .............................. 33
County Mayo 1585 ................................ 36
Culmore 1825 ................................... 117
Dublin 1722 ..................................... 70

Dublin c.1790 ................................... 79
Dublin c.1800 ................................... 83
Dublin 1801 ..................................... 84
Dublin 1803 ..................................... 86
Dublin 1803 ..................................... 86
Dublin 1803 ..................................... 87
Dublin 1814/15 ................................. 107
Dublin District 1828 ............................ 122
Dublin 1831 .................................... 125
Dublin 1837 .................................... 131
Dublin 1837 .................................... 131
Dublin 1843–44 ................................. 135
Dungannon c.1609 ................................ 57
Dunleary 1820 .................................. 111
Dunmore East 1832 .............................. 127
Enniskillen 1594 ................................. 47
Enniskillen District 1803 ......................... 88
Hollymount 1810 ................................. 99
Idrone c.1580 ................................... 35
Ireland c.1558 .................................. 22
Ireland 1567 .................................... 22
Ireland c.1580 .................................. 33
Ireland c.1610 .................................. 65
Ireland c.1759 .................................. 72
Ireland 1793 .................................... 80
Ireland 1803 .................................... 89
Ireland 1804 .................................... 94
Ireland 1810 ................................... 100
Ireland c.1846 ................................. 137
Ireland c.1865 ................................. 143
Kinsale 1637 .................................... 68
Kinsale 1691 .................................... 70
Kinsale c.1770 .................................. 76
Kinsale 1815 ................................... 108
Knockninny c.1609 ............................... 58
Knockninny c.1609 ............................... 58
Limerick 1587 ................................... 39
Limerick 1587 ................................... 39
Limerick 1803 ................................... 91
Lismore 1760 .................................... 75
Londonderry 1799 ................................ 81
Londonderry 1827 ............................... 122

Lough Swilly 1803 ............................... 91
Loughtee c.1609 ................................. 61
Lower Iveagh 1725 ............................... 72
Lower Malone 1840 .............................. 133
Mayo 1587 ....................................... 41
Meelick 1810 ................................... 101
Monaghan 1590 .................................. 45
Monaghan 1591 .................................. 47
Monaghan/Enislaghan c.1610 ....................... 67
Mulline c.1610 .................................. 66
Munster c.1572 .................................. 29
Munster c.1580 .................................. 30
New Ross 1803 ................................... 93
Newry c.1570 .................................... 26
Newry c.1570 .................................... 26
Newry c.1570 .................................... 26
Newry, Warren Point &
Rostrevor Railway, 1846 ......................... 138
Newton Hamilton 1821 ........................... 113
Omagh c.1609 .................................... 61
Oneilland c.1609 ................................ 62
Portrush c.1580 ................................. 34
Portrush c.1859 ................................ 141
Roscommon 1581 .................................. 36
Shannonbridge 1810 ............................. 103
Sligo 1589 ...................................... 42
Sligo 1821 ..................................... 115
Smerwick Harbor 1580 ............................. 36
Southwest Ireland 1837 .......................... 128
Spike Island 1803 ................................ 93
Strabane 1609 ................................... 62
Templemore 1826/31 ............................. 120
Tralee 1587 ..................................... 41
Tullyhaw c.1609 ................................. 62
Ulster c.1580 ................................... 30
Ulster 1602–3 ................................... 48
Ulster 1602–3 ................................... 51
Ulster 1602–3 ................................... 51
Waterford 1825 ................................. 118
Wicklow 1579 .................................... 30